IN-LINE SKATING MADE EASY

A Manual for Beginners with Tips for the Experienced

by

Martin Dugard

An East Woods Book

The Globe Pequot Press

Old Saybrook, Connecticut

For Matt

Photo Credits: Pages 1, 5, 23, 47, 74, 121 *bottom,* 139: photos by Geoffrey Fosbrook, courtesy Bauer In-Line Skates; pages 6, 95, 98, 99: courtesy Bauer In-Line Skates; pages 11, 20, 21, 109, 110, 115, 116, 119, 120, 121 *top:* photos copyright © Tony DiZinno; page 18: photo by R. J. Phil; pages 35, 65, 67, 83, 90, 94, 100: courtesy K2; all others copyright © 1996 Rich Cruse, RC Photo.

Library of Congress Cataloging-in-Publication Data
Dugard, Martin
   In-line skating made easy: a manual for beginners with tips for the experienced / by Martin Dugard
      p.   cm.   —   (Made easy series)
   "An East Woods book."
   Includes index.
   ISBN 1-56440-903-1
   1. In-line skating. I. Title. II. Series.
GV859.73.D84   1996
796.2'1—dc20
                                                                          96-19861
                                                                          CIP

Manufactured in the United States of America
First Edition/Second Printing

Contents

Foreword

I'll make a confession right now. I'm one of the "in-line hockey fanatics" that Marty Dugard mentions in passing in this book. Speed skating is what I try to do when I'm chasing a puck or ball—or if I'm being chased by an angry defenseman. Recreational skating is when I skate from my car to the parking lot where pickup hockey is being played. I'm not even sure I know what extreme skating is—I just think you have to be younger than me to do it.

Anyway, I know good in-line information when I read it, and this book is chock full of the inside stuff you'll need to become an in-line skater—whatever version you choose to be. Although Marty gears his advice toward the novice and intermediate in-line skater, there's no condescending tone from on high—Marty gives it to you straight. It's like taking a driving lesson from a friendly uncle who allows you to floor it on the straightaways instead of sweating it out while your father sits in the passenger seat and picks apart each left turn.

You can skip around in this book to find the information that petains to your specific in-line skating interest, be it recreational skating, speed skating, hockey, extreme skating, or skating with your kids. Just don't skip those important early chapters on proper equipment and safety! As a matter of fact, this book's section on "Protection and Why You Need It" should be required reading for every in-line skater. I always wear a helmet, knee and shin pads, and gloves when I play pickup roller hockey down at the beach in Santa Monica, California. I wear the helmet in honor of a buddy of mine who tripped, fell backward, and fractured his skull. He survived, but he spent over $8,000 on doctors who put him back together. Wear the gear—it's just the smart thing to do.

Exhaustive but not exhausting, this book should have a very short shelf life. By that I mean that it probably won't sit on a shelf much because you'll refer to it often as you're learning new and different techniques. And though I'm not an authority on other aspects of in-line skating, as a hockey fanatic, I can tell you that the hockey section is very helpful and the information is right on.

Marty advises you to break your big goals into small, attainable steps, and I think that's wise advice. "Practice makes perfect" is an old but true adage. Keep skating and you'll improve in no time.

See you on the parking lots soon—oh, and don't forget to bring your hockey stick!

Richard Graham
Editor
InLine Hockey News

Acknowledgments

Writing a how-to book is something I'd never attempted before this effort, so I must give thanks to several people who walked me through, reassuring me from time to time when I walked away wondering if the tone and subject matter were being addressed properly.

On a professional level, my editor, Laura Strom, deserves some sort of medal for patience. The manuscript was more than a tad late, and I admit somewhat sheepishly that I underestimated the breadth of the endeavor and promised it a full three months before I was able to produce it. Laura was obliging at times, firm at others, and always a joy to work with. My thanks for her calm stewardship.

Also, thanks to Valerie Thiel of *CitySports* magazine, who provided me with the appendix information. Also, to Tony DiZinno and Rich Cruse, for their wonderful photos and friendship.

On a personal level, I must thank several people. First, to my wife, Calene, who provided her usual high level of inspiration throughout the project, especially in the first few months, when words came out in dribs and drabs instead of a stream-of-consciousness torrent. To my boys, Devin and Connor, who are well on their way to becoming better in-line skaters than me and who regularly invaded my office to take me outside to skate. To my brother Matt, my long-time skating partner in the days when our wheels were attached to skateboards instead of in-lines. By virtue of his sheer recklessness, he convinced me that several difficult maneuvers I was afraid to try weren't so difficult after all. That philosophy has followed me ever since, in all I do.

And last of all, to my Mom and Dad, who let Matt and I build a half-pipe in the front yard when we were teenagers, then let half the neighborhood come over to skate it. I think they always hoped something other than just a few scrapes and bruises might emerge from the lessons learned on that plywood eyesore. Well, something did, Mom and Dad. This book.

1

IN-LINING: IT'S NOT AS TOUGH AS IT LOOKS

You've seen them out there. Maybe, as you watched them glide about, you doubted that it was within you to ever be one of them. They're fit, with muscle tone up and down their legs and abdomens, and skinny waists that appear as if they slimmed into place without a whit of hard work. Strangely, they smile, which isn't a normal endeavor when people exercise. And they certainly don't look like they're in a hurry to get done, because, let's face it, they look like they're having a really good time.

Maybe, as they flowed here and there so effortlessly and flawlessly, something deep inside you wished that they'd crash, just to make life interesting.

"They," of course, are in-line skaters. Anymore, they're not just the local schoolkids who haven't yet procured a driver's license. They're not only the superfit or the supertrendy, and they're not just ex–hockey players looking for a fix, nor skateboarders, nor skiers seeking off-season fitness. Actually, they're all of that, plus much more. In-line skaters come in all ages these days, from toddlers to grandparents. People worldwide have come to realize that in-line skating is a good way to get in shape, stay in shape, have a good time doing it, and experience the heady rush of speed now and then. Speed, of course, is different from fun, because the potential for calamity is that much higher. Speed junkies will tell you that the adrenaline rush alone is enough to warrant the occasional scraped knee or bumped noggin, but that's another story.

The goal of the new skater should not be to pursue recklessness. (At least not initially. If you choose to pursue "extreme" skating at

Skating: Think of it as a relaxing walk in the park.

some point in the future, wait until you've mastered the fundamentals of in-lining and can feel at home and in control on your skates at all times. There's a world of difference between the kind of recklessness that takes place when you know what you're doing—controlled recklessness—and the out-of-control stuff that will get you and others hurt.) The goal should be instead to pursue the ideal of self-development.

I remember talking to a friend who took up in-line skating for a related reason: to rise above the level of mediocrity he noticed was engulfing his life. Instead of dreaming big and taking a lot of chances, like when he was in his twenties and even high school, my friend had settled into a life of humdrum daily occurrences. In-line skating was a small step outside his daily comfort zone. In the comfort zone, he felt trapped and complacent, but secure. Nothing particularly bad happened in his daily life, but nothing particularly exciting either. In-line skating became the first step of many that he ultimately took to make his life the more fulfilling frontier he had imagined when younger. His efforts have been wildly successful, and he now professes to a better relationship with his family and a greater degree of happiness in his profession. Sometimes it's something simple like introducing the unknown variable of a new adventure (in this case, in-line skating) to make a profound change in people's lives. Wild things happen outside the comfort zone.

I don't see in-line skating as the be-all and end-all, guaranteed to promote personal well-being. But I am amazed by its popularity, and I feel that this unlikely growth may be a barometer of how something as simple as pursuing this great new sport has found its way into the national subconscious. Right now, it's just worthwhile to remember that in-line skating is a great sport and it's here to stay. A report released by the National Sporting Goods Association in July 1995 reported that sales of in-line skating equipment would soon eclipse that of Little League baseball gear. Not that anyone wants in-lining to supplant the national pastime—or really believes that it ever will—but the undercurrent of that report was clear: We are entering a new era. Traditional sports like baseball and football are about to be joined by a new legion of sporting events centered around in-line skating.

A Short History Lesson

It's pretty cool, when you think about it. It wasn't that long ago that the only sports anyone paid any attention to were spectator sports. The idea was—and this is a notion that persisted until the late 1970s—that only professional athletes and Olympians should engage in anything more lively than touch football or a game of racquetball.

But then came the running boom. Suddenly, men and women the world over saw that they could participate in a sport—running—and get genuine enjoyment from the daily act of physical exertion. What's more, they began stretching the parameters of what they were able to accomplish. People who couldn't run a hundred yards were soon running a mile, then a 10K race, then—incredibly—a marathon. Ever since the messenger Phiddipides dropped dead after running history's first marathon (he was delivering news of a battlefield victory to the people of Athens, and after delivering the message, "Rejoice, we conquer," he keeled over and died), that had been the ultimate standard of human pain and suffering. It was considered an arena too extreme, too utterly grueling to be contested by any other than elite endurance athletes. But the running boom changed all that. Ordinary people doing extraordinary things became commonplace, and once the word got out that running a marathon was within the realm of doable possibilities, the world of participatory sports went wild.

The running boom got everybody in on the action.

It became the strangest form of phenomenon—a country, then a world suddenly gone mad for the idea of exercise, in fact, grueling exercise, the kind that was painful enough to make participation its own odd kind of reward. Thousands upon thousands of people began filling the streets of places like New York, Boston, Los Angeles, and London to endure, to persevere, to conquer. "Finishing is Winning," while an oxymoron to many, became the battle cry of this new age of exercise. The idea of crossing the finish line first, which was the central idea behind athletic participation—indeed, the singular motivation—became supplanted by the idea that stepping across at all was good enough. Anyone with the will to finish and the commitment to training could do it. While pundits predicted that exercise was destined to become just another outrageous fad that people glommed on to, like dieting, such wasn't the case because exercise wasn't only about losing weight, it was about self-empowerment. The masses ran because it made them feel good about themselves.

Not everyone stuck with running. Exercise is a very singular, subjective experience. While some folks crave the solitude and tranquillity of a long run in the forest, others need to be around people or to be a part of a team. Running experienced an inevitable decline in participation—once something becomes a fad, it's only a matter of

The start of the Hawaiian Ironman, a race that's one of the greatest examples of normal human beings finding out how much they can accomplish with dedication and preseverance.

time before it becomes passé—but the world didn't stop exercising en masse. It simply turned to other activities. Aerobics boomed, and health club memberships soared. Swimming and cycling attracted a huge following, as did other niche sports like cross-country skiing and weight lifting. It got to the point that running a marathon became almost commonplace. The Ironman triathlon came about for that very reason. Merely running a marathon wasn't tough enough, the reasoning went. For it to be a worthwhile challenge, it would have to be accompanied by other extreme endurance events, like swimming and cycling. The result: a 2.4-mile swim, 112-mile bike ride, then a full marathon run (the story goes that one early Ironman competitor brought a sleeping bag to the starting line with him that first year—he thought the event was to be contested over three days instead of one). So out of the simple confidence building engendered by the running boom, a whole society was plugged in to fitness.

The growth in niche sports diffused the focus, however. No single sport captured the imagination of the general populace like running had during its heyday. Meanwhile, in Minnesota, an invention was being fashioned that would change all that. Two brothers in Minneapolis were applying skateboarding technology to an existing roller skate that featured all four wheels lined up single file. By replacing their antique steel wheels with the urethane slicks that skateboarders depended on to grip the vertical walls of pools and pipelines, Scott and Brennan Olson—who had an affinity for hockey—found that they could get around on dry land just as if they were on ice skates. They called their skates Rollerblades, and by the late 1980s, they had found their niche market of participants. For the first time since the running boom, there was a sport that encompassed almost every age group and demographic indicator. America, and soon the world went crazy for in-line skates (the Olson brothers sold their patent for $100,000, not knowing that in-lining would soon become nearly a billion-dollar industry).

The reason for in-lining's popularity? Accessibility, mostly. Like running, you don't have to be superfit or obsessive about conditioning to enjoy the benefits. People also found that they could get out and roll around without spending a fortune on equipment, which is another noteworthy comparison to the simplicity of running.

But perhaps the most important reason in-lining took off exponentially was that the fear of falling was largely removed. The introduction of better, safer pads and helmets made injuries a less regular part of in-lining. Early in its development, in-lining was compared often with roller-skating. And when people thought of roller-skating, they thought of being twelve years old at the local roller rink, skating around in circles, or they recalled childhood memories of trying to maneuver up and down the sidewalk in front of their home while wearing clunky metal clip-on skates. But more than all that, they thought of falling down. Spasticity atop wheels is more common than control, and everyone who ever put on a pair of roller skates sooner or later ended up with a scraped knee or a bruised something-or-other. Shrewdly, the sales of in-line skates were tied to an admonition that safety should come first. Pads for every joint and damageable surface were offered, and people wore them. They didn't fall down any less than they did while a child on roller skates, but the outcome was far less traumatic and thus less memorable. It's like touching something hot. The first time you touch it, the memory of the pain becomes so intensely embedded that you think twice before touching that object again, even if it's not hot. By taking the pain element out of skating, the element of pleasure—which was the part of skating that kept people coming back—become the overwhelming sensation. If something makes you feel good, you'll keep doing it again and again. Pads made in-lining feel good.

Thinking About Trying In-Line Skating

The spasticity factor is still present even in in-line skating, but that's remedied by the old adage of "practice, practice, practice." In-lining is not something that comes naturally to most people, but it's most definitely doable. There's a perception—and I'm not sure I know where this comes from, but I have a clue, as I'll explain momentarily—that in-line skating is a difficult sport. Nothing could be further from the truth. It's one of the few undertakings that I know of where both adults and children can learn in an absurdly short period of time. Ironically enough, that, I think, is where nonskaters get the idea that in-lining is imbued with an impossible degree of difficulty. They see people of all ages skating so effortlessly, then leap to the assumption that attaining such expertise must be beyond their capability. They foresee a long learning curve filled with spectacular and painful crashes and quickly decide that perhaps their time would be better spent working on their short game, wandering around the mall, or maybe even lying on the couch, sipping a cold one.

It's really not as bad as all that. Taking the leap from nonskater to skater is more about accepting that there will be initial failures and awkward seconds when you won't be entirely in control. So what?

Nothing like a little effortless speed to spice up your life.

Everybody's doin' it!

Nothing in life should ever come entirely without trial. Those things that do are never appreciated. It's only by taking the time to invest yourself in an undertaking that you come to appreciate it.

By reading this book, you have decided to invest yourself in this learning process and to make the leap from nonskater to skater. I'm happy to tell you that there's nothing difficult or insurmountable about what you are about to undertake. That's not to say it will be easy—no skill that requires new levels of muscle memory ever is—but it's just that proficiency in in-lining can be yours with a bit of practice and patience.

Accept the fact that you will fall and that invariably your fall will occur just as the neighborhood kids effortlessly skate by, alternately leaping from curbs, dodging cars, and skating backwards without a second thought. Embarrassing moments like those will pass once you learn to center your weight and get in sync with your skates, making them just as much an extension of your body as you would a tennis racket or pair of skis, which won't take long. When that happens, you don't need to think about what you're trying to do, you just do it. Is there a turn coming up? Then take it. Is there a rock in your path? Leap over it or go around it. Once you get comfortable on skates—and you will—that control and effortlessness you now see in others will be yours. It won't take long. Like I said, in-lining's a pretty simple sport.

Let's go back a moment to the part about falling down and suffering, which is probably the number one phobia surrounding in-line skating. Handled properly, it's not something you need to waste an ounce of energy worrying about. I'll stress throughout this book the importance of proper safety equipment for several reasons, most notably that safe skating is the best form of preventing injury that I know of. But another side of that same coin is that wearing proper safety equipment will heighten your enjoyment of in-line skating by taking away much of the fear factor. Armored in elbow pads, knee pads, wrist guards and a helmet, you'll see that falling is a pretty painless experience. Once you've been through it a few times, you'll stop worrying about falling and start focusing your energies on the process of becoming a better skater.

I like in-lining quite a lot, but I'm not the kind of guy who will go so far as to say something like "In-lining is my life" or, worse, "In-lining is life." That's a bit much. But I do appreciate the symbolism of the sport and the metaphor of balance that runs through it: balance, as in keeping your weight over your skates; balance, as in learning to control your body while rolling forward at speed; and most of all, balance, as it pertains to life. In-line skating is not a sport that will overwhelm you with the need for hours of technique adjustments or training. It is a lifestyle sport, one that will easily incorporate itself into your day, bringing both exercise and stress relief. Balance is what I feel makes in-line skating one of the fastest-growing sports in the world. It's something people can learn easily, practice often (and everyplace), allot very little time to yet still receive its benefits, and enjoy for the practical aspects of fitness and stress reduction.

As you begin working your way through this book, learning the fundamentals of skating and the minutiae of skate composition, try to keep the concept of balance in mind. It will make the sport that much more enjoyable.

Setting Goals

The purpose of this chapter is to help you define what it is you want from in-line skating. That doesn't mean that you have to make a lifetime commitment to skating. It's more a matter of helping you define what your mental expectations are from in-line skating. Once you've done that, it will be easier for you to chart the learning curve you'd like to follow. By knowing where you want your learning journey to end, the process of defining the beginning and middle will be easier. In other words, if you want to be an in-line hockey player, then begin visualizing yourself in that role now—even before you begin to skate. Once you begin in-lining, the regular visualization of that goal will help you cultivate the skills (such as tight turns, heads-up skating, and skating within a group) necessary to become proficient.

That Awful Word

Goals. I realize the term *goals* is something people often buy in-lines to avoid—goals being synonymous with work and personal growth, in-lines being synonymous with mindless fun—but I think that in the back of your mind, you already know what you hope to get out of in-lining. Maybe you haven't told anyone else what that is, because, well, you don't want to get laughed at, or you're afraid you'll never become that type of skater anyway, so why bother sticking your neck out by spouting off a set of preposterous goals?

Rest assured, I'm not going to suggest that it is now time to put this book down, grab a nearby loved one, and ramble into that person's ear about self-fulfillment, self-realization, and personal growth as they apply to you and your in-line skating plans. If that were the case, this book might become a sequel to *Zen and the Art of Motorcycle Maintenance,* and that is not the case. However, this *is* a time to put the book in your lap for a moment and think about where you would like to be in a single year as an in-line skater. Let your mind really soar here, because you won't be sharing this with anyone but yourself. Do you want to become the Wayne Gretzky of the pavement? Or, more realistically, do you simply want to learn a thing or two about in-line hockey and then build that knowledge over time so that you can play in pickup games or in a league?

Do you want to lose a few—or a lot of—pounds? Maybe enough so that you could skate for a really long time without feeling winded and without your quadriceps screaming at you for all the abuse? Or maybe enough that you can look in the mirror and say with certainty that you possess total body tone?

Do you feel a burning desire inside to race, to lace up those skates and haul down the pavement without a care in the world?

Do you want to learn to pull air off the vertical section of a half-pipe? Grind? Fakie? (Don't worry—you'll know what all that means by the time you're finished with this book!)

Whatever it is you hope to achieve from in-line skating—and I think you already know what it is—admit it to yourself now, and tailor your skating development goals in that direction. Why? Well, beyond developing necessary skills for each type of in-lining, it's also important to know enough about the various types of skates that when buying time comes, you can make an informed decision.

If you know the direction you'd like to go with your skating, start paying particular attention to that aspect of skating now, and keep on following the information relevant to that type of skating as it appears throughout the book. By beginning with proper skate selection—and this may be a process that starts with one type of skate, then escalates into another in a year or two—you'll be buying a tool that will help you optimize the development of the particular skills suited for whichever direction you'd like your skating to take. Also, keep in mind that for whatever reason you have chosen to take up in-line skating, there is most definitely a skate for you.

A Step-by-Step Method of Setting Your In-Lining Goals

1. *Define what you would like to accomplish.* Hint: Avoid goals that depend on subjective outcomes. Make them quantifiable and objective. If your goal is to lose weight, don't make your goal "I

want to tone my muscles through skating," because you might never tone them to your satisfaction. Instead, say, "I would like to lose 2 inches off my waist" or "I would like to lose 10 pounds."

2. *Imagine a time frame (a month, a year) in which to accomplish your ultimate goal.* You might say, "I would like to learn to skate backwards." OK, how long until you feel you can do that? Set a reasonable time goal, not one that will lead to frustration by being too rigid or unattainable.

3. *Set intermediate goals.* If the ultimate goal is to play professional in-line hockey, then intermediate goals for a brand-new skater might be to learn to skate, then learn to skate with a hockey stick, then learn to shoot, and so on. By breaking a far-off goal into smaller bits and pieces, it becomes manageable. More important, motivation stays constant when you can measure forward progress. It's hard to get motivated if your goal is too far away to touch.

4. *Once you achieve a goal, set a new one.* It's what will keep you constantly growing, both as an in-line skater and as a person. Always keep trying to be your best, and avoid complacency.

I find that it helps to keep your goal written down someplace that you can see them (but preferably not where other people can see them; goals should be a private thing) and refer to them on a daily basis. A few years ago I remember having time to kill on a long flight, so I pulled out a scrap of paper and agonized over my goals for the year. Where did I go? What were those dreams I wanted to work on? Where did I see myself in ten years? Believe me, I thought long and hard before setting pen to paper. When I was done, I was proud that I had defined my ambitions for the near future and felt confident that I could set forth with a greater sense of purpose to my daily activities. Just to make sure I looked at them constantly, I stuck them inside my Day Planner. Unfortunately, I stuck them near the back and never once thought to glance at those goals. Time passed and I forgot I'd even taken the time to write them down. At the end of the year I happened to stumble across them and felt somewhat chastened to note that some of the items that seemed pressing back in January had never been accomplished. In fact, I hadn't even worked on them. The moral here is to put those goals someplace your eyes will glance toward every day, or at least every week.

Moving On

Beginning with basic skate terminology and construction knowledge in the next chapter, we'll march through how-to fundamentals and into advanced skating skills. I can't overemphasize the importance of taking your time while learning. Read ahead if the mood strikes, but don't attempt movements your mind and body—and they are linked in in-lining, one always convincing the other that the impossible is possible—aren't ready for. I would advise, as always, that you practice, practice, practice. As I said earlier, there are very few natural skaters. Those effortless moves you see on the sidewalks and playgrounds of your city are invariably the result of hard work.

But look, don't beat yourself up if a particular maneuver escapes you. In-lining is supposed to be fun. It's a great time to let the mind wander and the muscles relax. I believe that once something as patently playful as in-lining starts to become work, then its function as a healthy extension of your life is over. So don't let skating become a grind. Enjoy. Play. Practice. Then play some more.

2

A SKATE FOR EVERY PURPOSE

Buying the Skate that Matches Your Goals

I remember reading a how-to book on skateboarding several years ago, and when the chapter on how to purchase the proper equipment came along, I skipped right past it because I had no intention of buying equipment for quite some time. Well, time went by, and I noticed I'd been buying equipment for this sport in bits and pieces. You know, a set of wheels here, a pair of bearings there. I think that is how most people purchase gear. Anyway, I noticed that I'd actually had to reacquire several items because I'd made poor selections. When I later reread the how-to book, I was surprised to find that I could have avoided this expense by reading the nuggets of information offered.

No, purchasing in-line skates isn't a prerequisite for learning how to skate (though, obviously, it is necessary to have access to a pair of skates), so don't skip right over the rest of this chapter if it's not your plan to rush right out and buy new skates today. It's my belief that if you experiment with, and find yourself taken with, in-line skating—whether you own your own skates or not right now—there will come a time in your skating career when you'll want to purchase a pair.

In-lines are like a car in many ways. When you first learn to drive, it's OK using someone else's car to get around town. But once driving becomes part of your lifestyle, well, that's when the natural desire to acquire creeps in. And purchasing a new pair of skates will be much easier once you know a thing or two about skates.

If you still need convincing that a little knowledge about skate selection is a good thing, consider this scenario: You find yourself at

Whatever your passion, there's a skate for you.

a cocktail party. Somehow the conversation has spun around toward the unlikely—but very trendy—subject of in-line skating, with an emphasis on skate specificity (again, we're talking about an unlikely, but entirely hypothetical situation). You have two options: either beg off and make your way back to the bar, or hang in there and impart the wealth of knowledge you will soon possess about in-line skates. In anticipation of times like that, it's my belief that the Proverbs quotation "Wise men store up knowledge" is appropriate. I think it's worth storing up a little knowledge about in-line skates, just on the premise that a little trivia can go a long way.

With that in mind, let's begin by defining the term *skate specificity*. It is simply the application of a specific skate to a specific type of skating: hockey skates for in-line hockey, recreational skates for recreational skating, speed skates for speed skating, and so on. Again, that's why I think knowing what you hope to attain in your in-line future is important now, before you even begin skating. Specific skates, specific application, specific skating skills.

For many people, when buying a new pair of in-line skates, there's a tendency to look more at price than design because, for the uninitiated, all in-line skates can look alike and—not knowing what constitutes a good skate or a bad skate—the buyer may conclude that the only way to get the best skate on the market is to purchase the most expensive model in the store. What such individuals do in a situation like that is assume two things: (1) the most expensive skate is the best, and if that's what they're looking for, that's what they'll buy, and (2) the cheapest skate is the worst, which means it should be purchased either as a gag gift or as an inexpensive way of satisfying an inner craving for in-lines. They see wheels and boots and buckles and shiny plastic and price tags, nothing more. The distinctions that make each model of in-line skate different are lost on them, just as makes and models of automobiles are lost on those who don't pay much attention to cars. But, as with cars, there are huge differences between types of in-line skates—differences that could drastically affect how you skate, where you skate, and why you skate.

Purchasing the most expensive skates in the store is not necessarily the answer. Yes, there are very good, very expensive in-lines. Likewise, there are some cheap little toys being passed off as in-lines, when, in fact, they are a mere caricature. The key difference in in-lines has less to do with price than it has to do with specific applications. In-line skating has gone beyond being a roller-skating–type sport, where simply skating around in a circle is considered satisfactory achievement. Now, in-line skating encompasses extreme skating, hockey, distance races, and even dancing. It's not only important, it's crucial to know which type of skate (and there is a different one for each of the listed disciplines) is appropriate for the type of skater you hope to become.

The Parts of an In-Line Skate

Before discussing the different types of skates, with all their intricacies, let's break down their component structure to give you a better idea of what you'll be looking at.

The Frame

This is the skate's chassis, responsible for holding the wheels in place. It's generally constructed of metal, nylon, or plastic. A good rule of thumb is that the stiffer the frame, the better the skate. Long, five-wheeled frames are favored by speed skaters, but skates with five wheels are only good for racing, due to their inability to either turn or stop quickly. Midlength, four-wheeled frames are the chassis of choice for both recreational skaters and roller hockey players, as they offer the speed and handling required in those disciplines. Three-wheeled skates are neither fast nor stable.

The Boot

The boot sits on top of the frame. Although some manufacturers make a one-piece boot and frame called a monocoque, generally the two are separate components. Most boots are injection-molded from either polyurethane or polyethylene, just like ski boots (in fact, several ski boot manufacturers own in-line skating companies as well). The fastening is also reminiscent of ski boots, with buckles the current rage, replacing the laces that once dominated the in-line market (laces, however, are still popular for racing skates and hockey skates). Another ski boot similarity: There's a liner inside—known as the inner boot—to cushion your foot against the hard frame. The inner boot also acts as a stabilizer to prevent excessive lateral movement that could cause torque or impair your skating technique.

If you prefer superior fit and less weight, consider hand-stitched boots. Made of ballistic nylon, leather, or plastics, they're more expensive but form to your foot like a good running shoe, which makes the need for a liner superfluous. Whichever type of boot you choose, look for lateral support, ease of forward lean, and ventilation. A quick explanation of each:

Diagram of an In-Line Skate

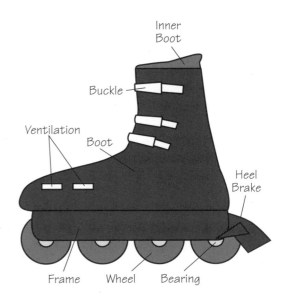

Lateral support. While skating, the body moves in a side-to-side lateral direction, instead of a linear pattern. The knee, surprisingly, doesn't feel a negative effect. What does suffer from all that swaying are the muscles of the ankle, lower leg (primarily the shin), and foot. This effect is increased when the boot ceases at a point just above the ankle. Speed skaters, however, don't usually experience this problem because they have the talent and experience to balance their body weight perfectly over the center of the wheels, thereby minimizing the lateral stress on the shin, ankles, and foot. In fact, these muscles, working in concert, are what allow the speed skater to be so efficient.

For a regular boot, make sure the liner is snug around your lower calf. Your ankles should be solidly supported, ensuring that the focus of a bad turn won't allow them to get turned or sprained suddenly. A good rule of thumb is to try on boots and stand up. If the skate feels "tippy" in the ankles—that is, if you feel a wobbling sensation instead of rigid support—then your boot may not offer enough lateral support.

Ease of forward lean. While skating, you'll bend your body forward at three points: your waist, your knees, and your ankles. Each of these, you may be surprised to know, can be adversely affected

Cutaway view of proper forward lean

Cutaway view of improper forward lean

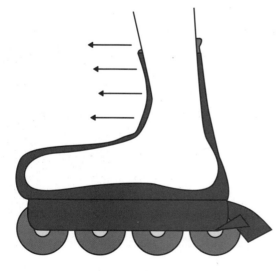

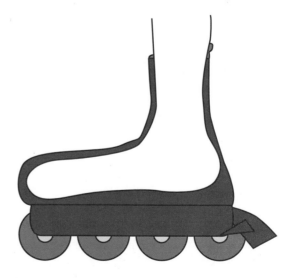

Note ankle flexion

Note heel lifted and pressure on forefoot because flexion is taking place there instead of at ankle by inflexible boots. It's a chain reaction, one best demonstrated by starting at the boot and working up. Let's say you buy a pair of boots that are a tad too rigid. You know they're too rigid because you are unable to lean forward at the ankles. It's like your feet and lower legs are encased in cement. Suddenly, because your ankles cannot lean forward, you find that, although you bend your knees to assist in the forward lean, the only thing that happens is that your waist is forced to bend and drop your body into a sitting position. In short, you are not in a position to skate.

How to look for good lean? You'll know it when you feel it. Like the lateral movement sensation, your ankles should feel snug inside your boots. If you can lean forward too much—say, to the point that your lower legs pass a 45-degree angle in relation to the ground— you'll find when you try to skate that the toes and the ball of the foot will try to do too much work, leading to Achilles tendon problems. If you can barely lean at all, you'll have that "stuck in cement" feeling I mentioned.

Proper ventilation. Ski boots lack ventilation because skiing is a cold sport. In fact, ski boot manufacturers add as much insulation as they can possibly get away with when manufacturing ski boots. Who wants to be known as the maker of cold ski boots?

The opposite is true of in-line skates. "Hot skates" is a phrase no company wants to hear about its product, other than as an exclamation (as in "Hot skates, dude!! Totally rad!"). There are two kinds of "hot" sensations that come with skating. The first is simply a lack of ventilation. No opening on the outside leads to a lack of air moving around inside, which leads to a sweaty foot. The second kind is when either a skate fits poorly or the skater has too many pairs of socks on, thus creating a "hot spot." Hot spots are caused by friction and eventually lead to blisters. The best way to prevent them is by purchasing a skate that fits, plain and simple.

The lack-of-ventilation issue can be avoided by selecting a skate that has holes in the sides. Simple, right? Well, not that simple. Too many holes causes a lack of structural stability. You want to purchase a skate that has the ventilation system plus a solid structure. It's hard to tell what's what, especially now that many manufacturers are try-ing to trim weight from skates—light equals fast—and are eliminating a great deal of structure from their boots. One manufacturer, for in-stance, has done away entirely with molded plastic on the portion of the boot covering the upper foot. Instead, it offers a complex lacing-and-buckle system.

How to pick the best ventilated skate that will support you as

Notice the ventilation holes at critical junctures on this boot.

you skate? Shop around, try skates on, and find one that feels right. This is such a subjective area that only you can be a good judge.

Wheels and Bearings

Wheels vary in hardness, diameter, and width. Harder wheels go faster than softer wheels, but softer wheels grip the road better. Big wheels (in terms of diameter) are preferred by most speed skaters because they cover more ground with less effort (I don't pretend to understand the physics of it, I just know that it works like that). The drawback is that they raise your center of gravity, imbuing you with that dreaded tippy feeling. Wider wheels are favored for hockey and stunt skating, while thinner wheels are better for speed and recreation.

Bearings also affect speed. They're assigned a rating by the Annular Bearing Engineering Council (ABEC) based on the engineering tolerances of their construction. Higher ratings indicate higher tolerances, and thus a faster ride. Most recreational skate bearings are rated ABEC 1 or 3, though some don't merit an ABEC number at all. Speed skates generally have bearings rated ABEC 3 to 5.

Keep in mind that the boot and the frame should be given greater consideration when purchasing skates because they are lasting components. Wheels and bearings wear out and need to be replaced. These aren't high-tech automobiles or computers that we're talking about, so don't feel as if you can't learn a little skate maintenance. Anybody can learn to change wheels and bearings.

You'll probably need an Allen wrench to do the job. Some manufacturers provide their own tool for removing wheels; some require a socket wrench; but an Allen wrench is the most frequently required tool. Simply unscrew the wheels from the frame, then remove them. For maintenance, wipe them down with a rag, then reverse the direction they're rolling. This will prevent one side from wearing more heavily than the other.

Before you put those wheels back in, however, use the Allen wrench to gently pry the bearings from your wheels. It's not hard—they pop right out. Wipe the bearings down with that rag. Or, if you get the feeling they've outlived their effectiveness (you'll know because they won't spin easily anymore, or you'll hear the bearings clicking against each other inside the sealed housing, thus indicating that all the fluid has leaked out), simply replace them with another set. Reverse the removal process to do this, and pop them back into place.

Then put those wheels back in—or replace them if the wear is

Wheels

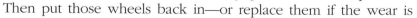

too great—and screw them tightly into position. Piece of cake. The whole operation for both skates will likely take less than half an hour.

Types of Skates

This is where a lot of people get tripped up by vanity. The temptation is to imagine themselves better skaters than they really are and buy a skate that doesn't fit their needs. For instance, a beginning skater has no business wearing speed skates. They're complex skates with little lateral support, no lining, five wheels—which means you can't stop on a dime in case of emergency—and absolutely no brakes. On top of that, the lower lateral support requires the skater to have a heightened sense of balance and feel for the skate. How do you get a feel for the skate? By skating, naturally. When a beginning skater purchases speed skates because he imagines himself as the Dan Jansen of the local parking lot, then a crash is most definitely in his future. On the other hand, if that same speed skater wanna-be puts his ego aside for awhile by getting the hang of recreational skates first, then trying speed skates, he's more likely to bring a greater number of skills to the fore when he crosses over.

Please, if you're a beginner, don't be embarrassed. Revel in it. Revel in the fact that you can fall down a lot and ask silly questions without people thinking you're obnoxious or inappropriate. And revel in the fact that good recreational skates, which is what every skater should learn to skate with, are the most comfortable skate money can buy.

If you're not a beginner, that's worth feeling good about yourself, too. You have the option of stepping into a niche skate (hockey, speed, dancing) or maybe upgrading into a top-of-the-line recreational skate. In this day and age, that can mean a true performance machine.

Again, don't let your ego get in the way when you buy your first pair of skates. Buy something comfortable and functional, something that you'll use. The appendix contains a list of reputable sources of equipment. Here's a breakdown on different kinds of skates you'll see at the local skate shop.

Recreational Skates

It's worth admitting right here and now that I'm aware that nine out of ten people buy in-line skates for no other purpose than rolling around the neighborhood on a sunny afternoon. That's a good thing, because this is definitely not rocket science. It's a fun sport, meant to maintain an effortless air, and rolling around the block can be a great way to raise the heart rate and purge your body of stress. Maybe, after you've gotten the feel for skating, you'll incorporate in-lining as a form of exercise into your workout routine, paying particular attention to things like anaerobic threshold, resting heart rate, hard/easy days, and a whole lot of other variables. But if not, it's certainly no big deal. In-lining's fun, and making it a discipline (and becoming a slave to that discipline, as sometimes happens with workout programs) can strip the sport of its enjoyment potential.

Let's go back to the original assumption: You bought your skates for no other reason than to roll around the block on a sunny afternoon. You don't care a whole lot about excessive speed. Rapid cornering, other than the kind that helps you dodge sudden obstacles, isn't something you've given a lot of thought. And you probably don't plan on learning how to skate on a vertical ramp or how to skate and manipulate a hockey puck at the same time. For you, there's a specific type of skate, known generically as a recreational skate.

Recreational skates are built with an eye toward comfort instead of high performance. They have a well-padded boot and an inner liner, buckles instead of laces. There's a heel brake to slow you down. Most obviously, there are four wheels. Why only four? Because four is the perfect number to stretch from heel to toe of an average foot. Because four guarantees stability at speed—not excessive speed, but the sort of speed you're likely to encounter on that roll around the block. And because four wheels turn rapidly, smoothly, and efficiently.

Recreational skates dominate the sales charts, so there's certainly no stigma in purchasing a skate with a generic description like "recreational." In fact, I think that every new skater should begin on a pair of recreational skates because they're the easiest to learn on (which means you'll get better, faster). Four-wheeled recreational skates can run the gamut from beginners skates to high-performance machines, with pricing to match.

If you find yourself dismayed when you go to the store to select that first pair of skates, not sure which is the pair that suits your abilities, remember that a top-of-the-line, high-performance skate (you'll know it both by its lean design and by its price tag) isn't what you want. Chances are, its finer points (such as aerodynamic design and venting) will be lost on all but the most advanced skaters, and you

Four wheels, sturdy construction, and not a hockey puck in sight—a sure sign of a recreational skate.

should wait until you've learned quite a bit more about skates and skating. Likewise, bargain-basement skates (you'll know these because they look more like toys than items of athletic equipment— cheap wheels, bearings that barely spin, dull esthetics) aren't enough skate for you, even if you've never skated a day in your life. Why? Because the wheels won't have the type of composition to hold you in the turns, the buckles will be poorly placed and can lead to Achilles tendon problems, and the boot and inner liner will foot poorly, making your skating experience one of blisters and throbbing feet.

Better to find a midlevel skate, one that feels comfortably snug when you first slip into it. Make sure the buckles hold your foot and ankle firmly. You'll know you've chosen well if you have trouble lifting your heel inside your boot. Such movement leads to a dependence on the ball of the foot to push off during the push-and-glide movement of in-lining. Done properly, as we'll discuss in a few chapters, the same movement incorporates all of the foot, not just the forward portion.

At this point, don't worry about the weight of the skate in determining its comfort level, because if your skates are comfortable, you'll wear them more often. If you wear them more often, you'll skate more often, and if you skate more often, you'll become a better skater. Once you become a serious skater (and you'll know when that hallowed day arrives because the sport will have become effortless to you seemingly overnight), you can rush back to the store and pick up a pair of high-performance skates to heighten that effortless feel. That's when you want to think about weight and disregard price (close your eyes as they ring them up—performance skates can be on the steep side), not before.

In the meantime, with that first pair of skates, try to arrange for a demo spin around the store or on the sidewalk out front before finalizing your purchase. Make it a point to see that your four wheels have a feel of both grip and ease during turns. After you skate, take them off and spin the bearings. They should be smooth and quiet and able to spin for an extended period.

Speed Skates

This is where you enter the land of five wheels. Just for fun, when you go to try on a pair of recreational skates, ask the salesperson if you might take a look at a pair of speed skates also. The first

Speed skates have a look all their own.

thing you'll notice is the longer frame and that fifth wheel jutting out in front of the toe. Speed skates, you see, are designed for maximum stability at high speeds, so that extra wheel is necessary. And if you chance to attempt a spin around the store, you'll probably notice that you seem to go a little bit faster than in recreational skates without really trying.

Why is that? For starters, there's a different wheel size with speed skates. Slightly taller, with a firmer consistency and less resilience, speed skating wheels are made to go faster. As a result, they give up a little in the traction area, which takes us back to that fifth wheel. It's not really necessary to have an extreme amount of traction with speed skates, because they have an enormous turning radius. Instead of microscopic pirouettes, speed skates are designed to carve long, gradual racing turns. These types of gradual turns, endemic mainly to speed skating's wide-open courses, are meant to carry speed through the turn. The fifth wheel, then, isn't a detriment as much as it is a hybrid element that fits perfectly into the world of speed skating.

Compare that with using a four-wheeled recreational skate in a speed skating environment. The four-wheeled skate would be a touch slower automatically, because the wheels are meant to provide traction and stability through tight turns, not speed. It's not as though the four-wheeled skate can't get up a good head of steam, but next to a serious speed skate there would be no comparison. In the turning department, the recreational skate would better allow you to make a tight turn (though not at speed).

Another item by which recreational skates and speed skates differ is the brake. In short, speed skates don't have one. Built for speed, they sacrifice any element that adds extra weight, and a heel brake is obviously an optional accoutrement when the skater is more concerned with making forward progress than slowing it. It's just as well. The act of stopping with a heel brake, which involves lifting the toe of one skate while dragging the heel brake, is harder to do with that extra wheel in front of the toe.

Speed skates are also built for linear movement. This means they don't make a great slalom skate, in case you're looking for a skate with which to practice dry-land skiing. Also, although speed skaters are deft within a pack of other skaters—able to weave and bob to avoid being tripped—the speed skate is a cumbersome device to develop that sensibility for beginners. Chances are, you'll be a hazard to both yourself and other skaters if you try learning to skate within a group on speed skates. Better to develop the skill on recreational skates, then transfer to speed skates.

In conclusion, don't buy a speed skate as your first in-line skate. The things you need to learn—the nuts and bolts of turning, stopping, skating within a group, and above all, getting at ease in skates—are best learned on recreational skates. They're made for a wider variety of skaters, and they're much more forgiving. I know some skaters for whom it's an ego thing to wear speed skates instead of recreational skates. They believe that the simple act of wearing fast skates makes them a great skater. I think learning on recreational skates makes an individual much more well-rounded.

Hockey Skates

A glance at traditional recreational skates shows an amazing resemblance to snow boots: hard outer shell, buckles instead of laces (or buckles and laces), midcalf design, padded and insulated inner boot. But as your eye moves through the racks of skates, you might notice a boot with a different look. It's probably black, with a white trim or frame. There will almost undoubtedly be laces. If you look closely, you'll notice that the bolts are flush-mounted, or arrayed snugly against the face of the frame, so that they won't catch on the floor during a tight turn. The boot is made of leather, like a shoe, and the boot's height isn't much more than a few inches above the ankle. There's no heel brake, which might look out of place on a four-wheeled skate. You might even remark to yourself that it looks like an ice hockey skate with wheels instead of blades.

That's because it *is* a hockey skate. Although I know they serve the specific purpose of tearing up and down the rink, stopping on a dime, and carving microscopic turns, I'd much rather skate around my neighborhood on hockey skates than any other type of skate. Why? They're incredibly comfortable. It takes awhile, but once that leather boot conforms to your foot, you'll feel as if you're skating in slippers.

That doesn't mean I'd buy hockey skates as a gift for a new skater. To start with, they're wobbly. There isn't much in the way of a conforming inner boot to hug your foot in the name of stability, and that low collar will make your ankles wobble for a few days until you get the feel of things. Hockey skates are for hockey players, plain and simple. They're not a bad skate for learning on, and I wouldn't actually deter anyone from making this choice (especially if you plan on making just one in-line skate purchase over the course of the next several years), but be warned that it's a tougher, more technical way to learn to skate. Your sense of balance will need to be more in tune with your skating technique, leaving less room for error.

Downhill skates. Note the sixth wheel for stability at high speeds.

Three-Wheeled Skates

If you're looking at skates with three wheels instead of four or five, and if you're even at the point where you're reaching for your wallet to make a purchase, I have one word of advice: Don't. With few exceptions, three-wheeled skates are toys. They are unstable at speed, designed to appeal to people who don't have a great deal of knowledge about skating (remember, there are those who think there are no differences among types of in-line skates), and invariably made of cheap materials.

There are some limited uses for three-wheeled skates. Their turning radius is tight, which makes for greater ease in performing intricate ballet movements. (I saw a dance company perform an entire routine on three-wheeled in-lines once, a perfect application.) If you're an average skater looking to learn an appreciation for skates, however, three-wheelers will not serve your purpose. Stick with four-wheeled recreational skates.

3

PROTECTION AND WHY YOU NEED IT

Protection. What a word. It conjures up images of being swaddled, content, taken care of. The world is full of mystery and intrigue, and the concept of protection seems designed to allay any and all fears about harm. To feel protected is to feel like no possible harm can come to you. In-line skating is one of those sports that begs for its participants to embrace the concept of protection. With it, people slide into their skates and leave their worries behind. Without it, the fear of falling can rob the sport of its joy. For some strange reason, many skaters feel that protective gear is an optional nuisance, that they don't need pads because pads look goofy (I'm the exact opposite: I think pads look as cool as or cooler than the skates on my feet) or that helmets mess up their hair.

Well, look, everybody needs a little protection now and then. It doesn't apply just to in-line skating. Pro football players wear helmets and pads. Baseball catchers wear face masks and chest protectors and use big mitts. Hockey players swath themselves in so much armor and padding that even a slap shot creates a mere bruise (a big bruise, but still just a bruise).

Beyond the realm of sports, you probably have an air bag in your car and a seat belt that you strap on before going anywhere. At home, you have a smoke alarm on the ceiling, railings on staircases, anti-skid substances on the shower floor, and that special rubber skirt inside your garbage disposal to prevent you from sticking your hand inside accidentally or being injured by bits of flying, already-chopped food.

As you can see, protection is what life is all about. Why risk an

No, this man is not a stalker, but you'll still want protection—in the form of helmet and padding—when in-line skating.

unnecessary injury? Why spend unwanted time in the emergency room? So before you step out of that store with your new pair of skates, take time to ponder another—highly necessary—purchase: protection.

Protection in the form of a helmet. Wrist guards. Knee pads. Elbow pads. These might seem like peripherals, expenses to be incurred at a later date due to their perceived frivolity or put off forever in the name of macho individuality, but there's nothing frivolous about breaking your elbow or fracturing your skull. And, even though it seems quite minor, there's nothing at all frivolous about scraping your knee. Think for a minute about your knees. Can you remember the last time you scraped them? Think back. You were a kid, probably. You cried a lot because it hurt a lot, right? There's nothing painless about having the cold, hard pavement (no matter how many times you fall, pavement will never, ever get softer) scraping away a layer of skin and drawing blood. Worse, you might have had a pair of your favorite pants on when you fell on that knee. To get to the skin, that pavement had to first rip a jagged, irreparable hole in that neat pair of pants.

Prevent all that. Wear knee pads. Wear a helmet. Wear wrist guards. You might even think about wearing hip pads (especially for beginners, hip pads can preclude some nasty, painful spills). You'll be glad you did.

I'm a good case in point. I have a history of clumsiness. Sometimes I think it's a miracle that I can skate at all, given my ability to fall down in a variety of creative and painful ways. I've battered my elbows in serious falls, scabbed my knees, and skinned my palms (and almost broken my wrist more than once). On one memorable occasion I crashed going about 30 miles per hour. My hands hit the ground so hard that my wedding ring flew off. My head bounced off of the pavement with such violence that my neck was stiff for two days. More ominously, my helmet cracked down the middle. But without it, I like to remind myself, that crack would have been down the middle of my skull. Obviously, I'm glad I was wearing my helmet that day. I've worn it every day since and taken to wearing all other forms of protection as well. It just doesn't pay to skate without padding—don't find that out the hard way.

Helmet

If you buy only one piece of equipment, buy a helmet. It's an old adage, but you can't replace your brain if you break it. Crazy as it sounds, most people who skate without a helmet eschew it because there's a certain amount of inconvenience to slipping one on: inconvenience in the form of messed up hair, a hotter head (which leads to some serious sweating on a hot summer day), and the added weight of skating with something atop your head.

When you think about it, though, those are all pretty lame excuses. Wear a helmet. Trust me, it's worth it. Helmets save lives.

Two of the most common methods of falling are falling straight forward and slipping backward so that the head bounces off the pavement. These are important facts to know, because you want to tailor your helmet purchase around these ideas. What should you look for in a helmet? The list is short: structural integrity, proper padding, a secure chin strap, and coverage for the front and back of the head in case of a fall. Let's go down the list item by item.

Structural integrity. This means don't buy a flimsy piece of plastic that looks and feels more like a toy than a protective device and that's going to shatter the minute your head caroms off the ground. You want to feel safe in the thing, sure that if you crash, your head will be protected. When shopping for a helmet, pick a few up, cradle them in your hands, and visually inspect the craftwork. Is it high quality? Does the helmet have a decent heft to it (and by that I don't mean weight, but just a good solid feel)? Most important, is it the kind of helmet you would want to be wearing in case of a crash?

Look for approval by the two national helmet-testing bodies, SNELL and ANSI. You'll see their symbols prominently displayed on the box and on the helmet if the helmet has passed muster (usually, this means stress tests involving either the helmet being dropped from a certain height or something heavy being dropped onto the helmet). Even if you do see the symbols, I urge you to conduct a few tests of your own. Drop it a few times. The salesperson shouldn't mind too much, if the store stands by its product. See how the helmet reacts to a fall. Does it make a solid sound as it hits the ground, or does it sound brittle? Does it seem to absorb shock, or does it bounce around awhile before settling down? These are important questions to answer, especially once you imagine the idea of your head inside, absorbing the same fall.

Proper padding. There are two basic types of helmets. One has a Styrofoam inner shell to protect the head, with small pieces of padding added to ensure a proper fit. The other type eschews the Styrofoam padding in favor of a "one size fits all" form of inner foam rubber padding.

Helmet—Cutaway Diagram

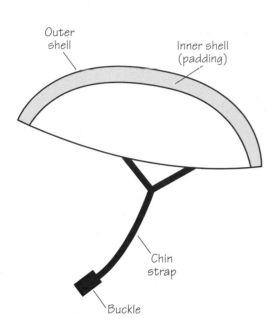

Outer shell

Inner shell (padding)

Chin strap

Buckle

Neither type is really better than the other. It's all a matter of personal comfort. What's important is that the padding exists and that it surrounds your head in a snug, protective manner. After you've dropped that helmet on the ground a few times, try it on to get a feel for how the padding system adjusts to your head. You'll wear that helmet more often if it's comfortable, instead of purely for safety reasons, so you'll want to make sure the helmet you buy is something that doesn't hurt your head (too tight) or float around so much that it drops into your eyes (too loose). Ideally, even without the stabilizing assistance of a chin strap, the helmet should fit securely in place. If it doesn't, try another size.

A secure chin strap. This is the thing that's going to keep your helmet from flying off if you crash, so you want to make sure that it's made of a sturdy fabric. Look for nylon mesh or some such material. These kinds of straps are solid and will probably outlast the helmet itself in event of a major crash.

As for the buckle, most helmets now offer the hard plastic type with a tongue-in-groove. It's a simple matter of sticking the tongue into the slot until a loud "click" can be heard, signifying that the buckle is securely locked into place. This type of buckle is secure enough that it won't come loose in any type of crash. It's important, however, to make sure that you adjust the buckle and strap properly.

What comprises a proper adjustment? The buckle should fasten snugly beneath your jaw, allowing enough room that two fingers can fit easily beneath the buckle and your skin. One good way to tell if the buckle is too tight is that you'll have a tendency to pinch yourself with the buckle each time you snap it shut. One good way to tell if it's too loose is that the buckle will swing around beneath your jaw, banging against your throat and chin as you skate.

Remember, the purpose of proper adjustment is that your helmet stays in one place on your head instead of shifting every which way. In the event of a crash, this adjustment will prevent the helmet from shifting too far forward, for instance, exposing the back of the skull to injury. Worse, a thoroughly absurd adjustment means that the strap won't affix the helmet to your head in any sort of permanent manner. Your brain bucket will fly off as soon as you bang the helmet against anything solid, which effectively negates the time spent choosing a close-fitting, well-built helmet.

Coverage for the front and back of the head. As I mentioned before, you're likely to crash in one of two ways: falling backward or falling forward. The physics of in-line skating means that your chances of tumbling laterally—to the side—are pretty slim. That means that if you take a severe tumble, the kind where a head injury comes into play, it's really nice but not absolutely essential to have your ears covered entirely. However, covering up the front and back of your head is a key element of skating. There's something inherently startling about slamming your head against the pavement that makes covering these areas of enormous importance. I don't think anyone wants to risk serious damage just because they chose in-line skating as their new form of exercise and relaxation.

When thinking about the front and back of the head, then, it's helpful to remember that there are two main types of helmet options available. The first is the more aerodynamic bicycle-type helmet, and the second is the football-type helmet (without face mask, of course), which has fewer aerodynamic qualities but covers the head more thoroughly. There are pros and cons to each. Both are SNELL and ANSI approved, so neither is unsafe. Both possess hard outer shells and offer sufficient padding on the interior. Both offer a number of vents in the shell to allow air to pass through. (An interesting point is that although the helmet will make you sweat, the forward motion of in-line skating causes air to pass through the vents, creating a type of natural air conditioning).

Here's where the differences begin. Bicycle helmets feature more padding on the interior, cradling your head a bit more. The drawback is that they cover less of the head, exposing a greater portion of the front and back of the head to injury. Proponents of bicycle helmets will tell you that, properly adjusted, their helmets will deflect a blow as well as or better than any other type of helmet.

Football helmets, while offering padding of a lesser thickness, come down to the eyebrows in front and to the base of the skull in back. In the event of a crash, these areas are well covered.

Which type is better? Neither, really. It's a matter of personal opinion. I skate in both, just because I have one of each and am prone to grab whichever is handy.

Padding

Knee Pads

Knee pads used to be a fairly generic item, interchangeable for use by wrestlers, basketball players, volleyball players, and anybody else who wanted to throw a layer of padding between their patellas and the cold, hard ground. But during the skateboarding resurgence

The two different types of in-line skating helmets.

of the late 1970s, when skaters moved their domain from horizontal to vertical by skating on ramps and the walls of empty swimming pools, it became obvious that regular knee pads weren't quite passing muster. For one, they did little to deflect the shock of slamming into the ground at speed. Wrestlers and basketball players rarely generate enough momentum to exceed 10 mph. Skateboarders were going two and three times as fast. As a result, their knees were getting bruised every time they took a spill, pads or not.

Another, more aesthetic, problem was that traditional knee pads were covered with either a cloth or an elastic substance. In the event of a crash, they tore. And once that cover tore, the padding inside was exposed. That padding, in turn, got rubbed away with each subsequent fall, until there was nothing left. The result was a knee pad with a terribly short life.

Then a company named Rector came up with a new idea: pads designed specifically for skaters. Not only did they offer a slip-on knee pad, with Velcro straps that could adjust tension around the leg (another problem with traditional pads was that they weren't made to

A good knee pad covers the knee as well as the area directly below the knee.

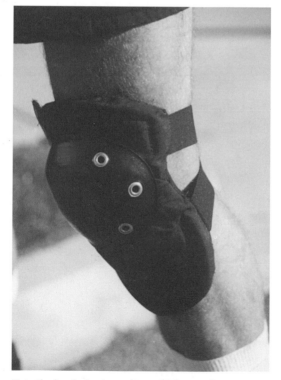

Note the hard plastic cowling, which provides extra shock absorption.

be worn over long pants, which skaters often favored), but they also featured a hard plastic shell that absorbed the weight of a fall. An ingenious side effect was that the blow was also deflected somewhat, because the hard plastic tended to slide on the hard pavement in event of crash. The proficiency level of skateboarders suddenly skyrocketed, as they were more willing to take chances on radical maneuvers, sure that their pads would protect them in the event of a fall.

Today those same pads are being used by in-line skaters everywhere (hockey players wear different pads, however; speed skaters tend to wear none at all. I mean it when I say that it's now possible to fall on in-lines and feel almost no pain. Knee injuries, especially, are pretty much a thing of the past for those who wear pads.

So what to look for? There are all sorts of pads and pad manufacturers on the market these days, so instead of shopping for a particular name brand, start by finding something your size. Pads come in small, medium, large, and kids' sizes. Be cognizant that you'll be wearing long pants sometimes. Other times, you'll be wearing shorts. For this reason I would avoid slip-on pads, which require you to remove shoes and socks (or skates and socks) to slip on and can feel constrictive with too much clothing, in favor of those that use Velcro straps to wrap the pad around the leg. These come on and off more easily and are instantly adjustable. One drawback is that they tend to slide around more than slip-on pads, but proper adjustment (and good Velcro) can allay fears about that.

You want the hard shell of the knee pad to fit comfortably over the center of your knee. In the case of a fall, that shell is what will absorb the stress, so make sure that it fits. Otherwise, the shell will tend to slip to one side in a fall, exposing your leg to the pavement.

That's about it. Buying knee pads isn't that tough. Just look for a pair that fits, make sure the construction looks and feels solid, and—most of all—make sure you wear them when you skate.

Elbow Pads

There's a sentiment that elbow pads are somehow not as important as knee pads, probably because elbow injuries don't happen as often as knee injuries. However, I feel that elbow pads are just as important as, if not more important than, knee pads. See, when you fall on your elbows—and although it won't be that often, it will invariably be memorable—you're most likely to be in a position where you're falling backward. That means that instead of a short, abrupt fall—which is the case with a knee-type forward crash—your elbows

Knee and Elbow Pads

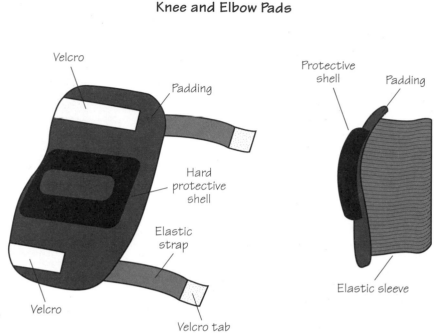

Elbow pads: an underestimated but very necessary protection for a vulnerable, exposed area of the body.

are absorbing more of a long, sustained drop because your elbows are positioned much higher on the body than your knees. Every time I've fallen on my elbows—and when I was learning to skate, that was where I invariably fell—I've gotten up sure that one or both elbows were broken. The elbow is a bony, exposed, pointed joint. It hurts—really hurts—to absorb the full weight of your body on those elbows in a crash.

So wear elbow pads. You'll be glad you did. When buying elbow pads, look for the same qualities as in knee pads—fit and construction. It's easier to try on elbow pads in the store than to try on knee pads, so feel free to slip on a pair. Again, if the salespeople don't like it, remind them that they're not going to be the ones paying the hospital bills if the pads don't fit.

Wrist Guards

As with knee pads, the evolution of wrist guards came from skateboarding. Tired of having their hands rubbed raw by falls, skaters began wearing leather work gloves to skate in. Those were nice, but they had a certain improvised air that took away from the professional, validated look skateboarders were seeking at the time. The solution was skateboarding gloves. Made of leather, with a thick

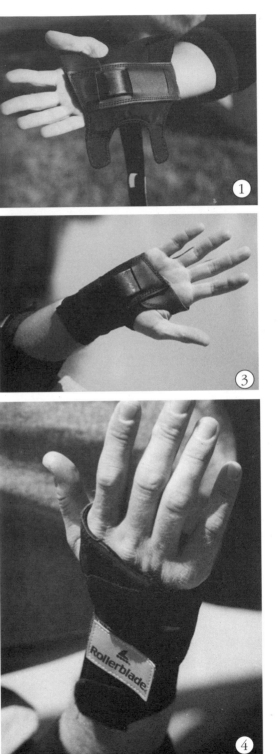

Slipping on a wrist guard: (1) Insert thumb in hole with plastic on top; (2) wrap Velcro band around wrist; (3) secure the two Velcro elastic straps; (4) the resulting security.

Diagram of a Wrist Guard

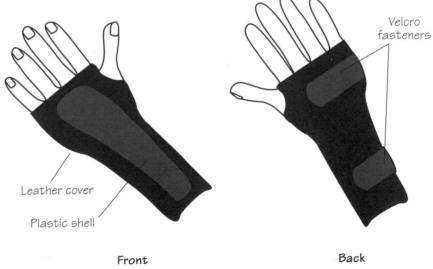

Velcro fasteners

Leather cover

Plastic shell

Front

Back

pad in the palm and a snug velcro wrist strap, they were perfect for preventing scraped palms and like distresses. There were a few problems, though. The gloves got very hot, very fast. Skateboarding, like in-lining, is an athletic sport. Heavy leather gloves, even those with ventilation holes, weren't made for that kind of abuse.

The other problem was more severe. During high-speed spills, skaters were finding that the fragile, six-bone network in the wrist, known as the carpals, became sprained or broken easily. Some took to wearing bowler's wrist guards to prevent such injury. Fashioned like a protective sheath, they wrapped around the lower portion of the hand and descended down the first third of the forearm. Within such protection, movement of the wrist was limited, but the chances for injury were minimized.

Well, somewhere along the line, someone decided it was a bright idea to combine the best features of a skating glove with the best features of a bowling guard. For added protection, a touch of knee pad technology was thrown in. The result: a cool (fingerless) glove/wrist guard with a hard plastic splint running down the front. The plastic was curved slightly outward—not enough to hinder normal wrist and hand movement, but enough to act as a shock absorber in the event of a fall. The wrist guards caught on. Once in-line skating became more popular than skateboarding, the use of the wrist guards grew even more because in-lining is a sport with a proportionately higher number of adults than skateboarding. And whereas having a cast is sometimes a cool thing if you're a younger skateboarder (badge of honor and all that), it's a passé hindrance to an adult. Nobody wants to hassle with the emergency room and the insurance bills. Nobody wants to wear a cast into the workplace. Nobody wants to fuss with a cast in the shower. Wrist guards to the rescue.

Hip Pads

This is one item of safety equipment I recommend only to the extremely accident-prone. The physics of in-line skating, with all that forward-directed movement, precludes many lateral crashes, meaning you won't ding your hips all that often—which isn't to say that you won't. And as with elbow crashes, those who have endured a serious fall on their hip remember it forever. There are some people who can tell you in detail about each and every time they've fallen on their hips, that's how memorable the pain from such a spill is. So if you consider yourself the sort to go down a little too often, or if you

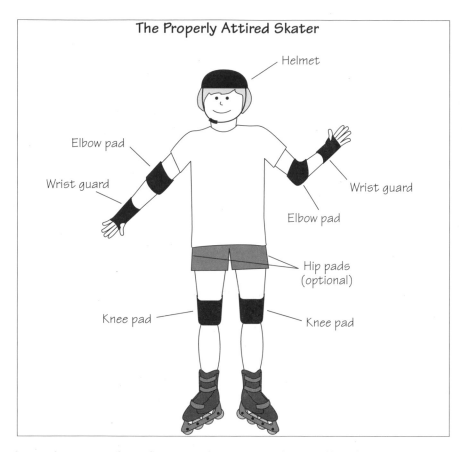

The Properly Attired Skater

Helmet

Elbow pad

Wrist guard

Wrist guard

Elbow pad

Hip pads
(optional)

Knee pad

Knee pad

have the type of profession where even the smallest hip bruise will set you back, then slip them on.

What are hip pads? Well, they're pads that cover your hips. What I mean to say is that while describing their function is easy, describing the appearance of hip pads is another story. Hip pads are something like sliding pads in baseball. They go on beneath your pants and form a protective layer around your hip bones. In some instances it is possible to buy pants with built-in pads (almost any snowboarding shop will carry them), though these can feel a bit bulky for skating.

Buy them if you want. Wear them if you must. Hip pads are the only element of safety gear that can actually detract from the pleasure of skating. Better safe than sorry, some will say, and I agree with that. If you have any inkling whatsoever that serious hip crashes are in your future, buy the pads and slip them on.

Other Types of Safety Gear

If you're so inclined, it's possible to skate fully armored. You could wear motorcycle leathers and a motorcycle helmet, for instance, and never once worry about bodily injury. But, really, that's a bit much. One of the joys of skating is conquering—or at least coming to terms with via expertise and body control—the concept of crashing. By wearing a helmet, knee and elbow pads, and wrist guards, you'll be more than adequately covered.

4

STRETCHING AND OTHER ESSENTIALS

Status check: You've bought your skates, or at least borrowed a comfortable pair in which to learn. You've got a helmet for your noggin, reliable elbow pads and knee pads for those irreplaceable, easily breakable joints, and hard-plastic wraparound wrist guards to prevent scrapes and carpal injury. So is it finally time to skate? Yes and no. Yes, you've got all the right equipment—and by now you know that in-lining is definitely a product-intensive sport—but your body, even if you're an accomplished athlete, isn't quite ready. You have to prepare it with even more of an eye to preventing injury than if you were preparing for a competitive athletic contest.

Never underestimate the benefits of flexibility.

In-line skating, you see, is a strenuous activity, and one not found in nature. It is not running, which we were all born to do. It is not walking. It is not basketball or baseball or football, all of which incorporate natural arm and leg movements. No, in-lining is none of those because the body was designed for forward locomotion, not lateral. It is none of those because none of them involve strapping narrow wheels to your feet, pushing yourself forward by angling one set of wheels to the side and sweeping that same leg out from the body. And none of those involve sweeping that leg away from the body while simultaneously and precisely tensing and balancing the muscle of the other leg atop these same narrow wheels. Meanwhile, your body is bent forward, your arms are swinging from side to side, you have armor covering every possible exposed area, and your brain is telling you with a growing sense of urgency that the entire enterprise is a crazy, nihilistic scheme destined to bring about grave bodily harm, a comprehensive list of which is sure to encompass massive contusions, profuse bleeding, and some sort of compound fracture. So without proper warning—and for future reference we will call this warning by its common name, a warm-up—your body will not take kindly to the new experience of in-line skating.

Once again, with feeling: Are you ready?

The Benefits of Warming Up

If in-lining had a kinesthetic cousin, it wouldn't be the obvious choice of snow skiing. It would be tennis. The definitive feel of both sports' lateral movements is roughly similar, the rapid forward and backward movements of a tennis match equate closely with the helter-skelter movements of an in-line hockey game, and there's an unnatural implement attached to an extremity, only with tennis it's a racket instead of wheels. And with time, in both sports, that unnatural implement becomes as natural a part of your body as your hands and feet.

Because of its intense, competitive nature, it is hard to imagine anyone going out to play tennis without a minimum of warm-up, and I think the same should go without saying for in-line skating. If

**Muscles Affected
by Skating**

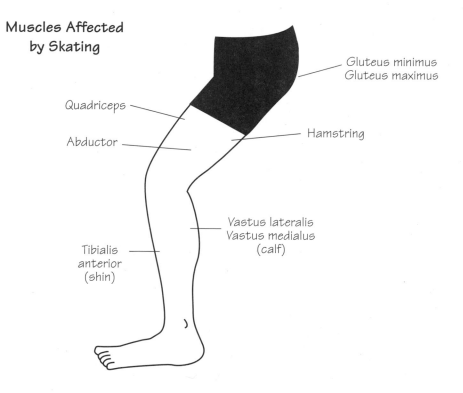

Gluteus minimus
Gluteus maximus

Quadriceps

Abductor

Hamstring

Vastus lateralis
Vastus medialus
(calf)

Tibialis
anterior
(shin)

anything, in-line skating should involve more warm-up. When tennis players fall down, it's generally nothing more than a minor slip, with no ensuing injury. When an in-line skater falls down, it almost always hurts—or at least it would without pads. Not to sound alarmist, but the body and the pavement are not naturally amenable to each other. And although pads absorb the shock that jars joints and bones, thus preventing injury, meeting the pavement is always a shocking experience. You can minimize the shock, however, by placing your muscles in a relaxed, pliable state.

Think of your muscles as rubber bands. A cold rubber band snaps easily when stretched. A warm rubber band can stretch almost forever without incurring damage. By warming up your muscles, you allow them the pliability to absorb a fall or react to the sometimes contortionist maneuvers that come from an unexpected fall. Again, this can't be stressed too much: Without proper warm-up, the risk of injury to in-line skaters is greatly increased.

Another, often unmentioned, side effect of warming up is muscle relaxation—you don't have to think about how to react, you just do it. One thing I'll keep repeating in this book is that the key to becoming a successful in-line skater is developing a total sense of relaxation atop your skates. It is important that your body feels loose and that your mind feels free to detach from the mechanics of skating to focus on peripheral details such as cars, uneven pavement, and—when you start skating in groups—the wheels and bodies of others. All of this involves relaxation, and the best way to get a feel for this intangible emotion—and it is an emotion—is by ensuring that your muscles are loose when you begin the act of skating. That involves warming up.

Now before you run off and do a hundred jumping jacks, then touch your toes fifty times, then drop for a round of push-ups, let's take a minute and rethink the concept of warming up. By its very definition, the warm-up is a time when you elevate the heart rate slightly, increase the flow of blood to muscles, and increase their temperature to prepare them for the movement of exercise. Traditionally, warming up meant a random series of semiviolent movements like jumping jacks and jarring stretches like toe touches. Despite the wealth of information showing how harmful they can be, many individuals still subscribe to these methods, not knowing that sudden radical exercise can easily lead to pulled or strained muscles. However, if you happen to be one of these people, and if this method of warm-up is something that has worked like a charm for you all your life, mentally fortified you for the workout ahead, and done nothing of consequence to your musculature; and if the thought of changing to a new regime makes your back stiffen with indignation, please feel free to turn to the next chapter and begin skating without fear. Every person's body is made differently, and if that is the technique that has worked for you in the past, then there is really no sense tinkering with success.

What I propose to the rest of you, however, is a simple and methodical plan to prepare your muscles and mind for in-line skating. Start, oddly enough (and before you put pads and skates on), with a brisk walk or, if you prefer, a short jog—not a long walk or jog, just five to ten minutes: enough to make it around the block once or twice; enough to mentally prepare for physical activity; and most important, enough to get the heart rate elevated and blood flowing to the muscles. In turn, the temperature of the muscles will increase slightly, making them less stiff (think rubber bands) and less likely to suffer injury during the next phase of the warm-up: stretching.

Stretching

The process of exercise is a constant, repetitive series of expansions and contractions of musculature. It's actually the same with all muscular movements, but exercises like in-line skating differ from, say, grasping a mug of hot coffee and lifting it to your lips, because (1) the expansions and contractions happen quickly, rhythmically, and repeatedly; (2) the body is being stressed, and (3) respiration is elevated as the body fights to acquire more oxygen. Not surprisingly, this process puts a strain on the muscles during the course of exercise (not so with a cup of coffee), which causes fatigue. Stretching is the process of slowly expanding a muscle to prepare it for the prolonged duress of exercise.

In-line skating is unique in that it works an extremely broad array of muscles. The legs, of course, bear the brunt of the action. The quadriceps, adductor, abductor, hamstrings, gluteus maximus, and muscles of the lower leg all play a part in orchestrating the push and glide. This area needs to be stretched thoroughly. The abdominal region needs to be strong to support the back, but supple to allow the diaphragm to expand and contract as the muscles take in oxygen (a tight diaphragm leads to that pain-in-the-side sensation known as a stitch). The arms and shoulders don't do much work beyond providing balance, but with their side-to-side movement affecting the torso, there's still a function being performed. Stretching the muscles of the upper body, while not as imperative as for the lower body, is still important.

When you stretch, do your stretches in whichever order you're most comfortable. I tend to start with the ones that can be done lying down, then finish with standing exercises, because it makes me feel as if I'm ready to spring into action the moment I'm done stretching. However, that's a personal preference, and if you want to reverse the order or go in no order whatsoever, feel free. It's also import to do whichever stretches work for you. The ones listed here are merely suggestions. Do them all or do just one; their purpose is to prepare you to skate. The point to remember is that you are limbering your muscles for the exercise to come. If you already feel loose on a particular day, or if some of them feel superfluous to you, skip the ones you don't feel you need. But don't skip any just because you're in a hurry to get started—you'll pay dearly for it later if you're not properly warmed up.

Legs

Calf stretch. With feet shoulder-width apart, stand two feet away, facing a wall (or a pole—so long as it's something solid). Keeping your heels on the ground, lean into the wall and support your weight with outstretched arms and your palms flat on the wall. You'll feel this stretch in the top portion of your calves.

Achilles tendon. Before you stop leaning into that wall, bend your knees. This means you've got your head leaning on the wall (supported by your arms), your feet flat on the ground, and your knees bent inward. This will shift the focus of that calf stretch to the lower region of the leg, especially that area around the back of your ankle and lower leg known as the Achilles tendon.

Hamstring stretch. We all know this one, but here let's do it with a spin. The idea is to reach down and wrap your hands around your Achilles tendon. However, don't keep your knees locked. Bend them slightly, just enough to keep them loose. If you can't reach your Achilles, reach down as far as you can. You may be able to only grab the back of your knees. That's fine. The idea isn't how far down you can reach, but whether or not you can stretch that hamstring.

Quadriceps. Stand on your right leg, with your left leg bent at the knee and raised, like a stork or a flamingo. Using your left hand, draw your left foot up behind you so that it touches your rear end. Now you should really look like a stork. The quadriceps, which is that group of muscles located on the front of your leg, should feel this stretch all the way from hip to knee.

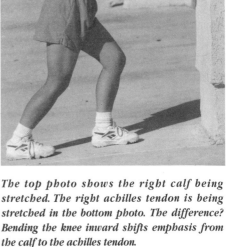

The top photo shows the right calf being stretched. The right achilles tendon is being stretched in the bottom photo. The difference? Bending the knee inward shifts emphasis from the calf to the achilles tendon.

Use this hamstring stretch to isolate the muscle of each leg, guaranteeing a thorough stretch.

Quadricep stretch   *Do these abductor stretches slowly for greatest effect.*

Think of a cat when stretching the upper back.

The key to this lumbar stretch is getting the knee all the way in beneath the diaphragm.

Abductor. This is the thin muscle running down the outside of your leg from hip to knee. Its job is to move the leg laterally away (*abduct* = to take away) from the body. To stretch it, stand with your feet shoulder-width apart, hands on hips. Bend your head and torso to the left, hold it there for a minute, then bend back and over to the right. Hold. Repeat this a few times.

Ankle. There are a few exercises you can do to stretch your ankle, but I've found the best isn't a stretch at all, but the simple act of sitting down on the floor, crossing one leg over the other and rolling your ankle with one hand. Repeat with the other ankle.

Back

Upper back. Get down on the floor on all fours. Tucking your chin down into your chest, arch your back upward like a cat. You'll feel the stretch in the top of your back and neck.

Lumbar region. This one's complicated, but great for stretching the lower back and buttocks. Lie flat on the floor, on your stomach. Extend your arms in front of you as far as they'll go. Now draw one knee up slowly until it comes under your body and is bent double beneath you. Hold that position. Repeat with the other leg.

Keep the head looking forward; twist no further than your body's mid-line.

Torso

Torso. Stand with hands on hips, feet a shoulder-width apart. Slowly twist your trunk to the left as far as it can go. Hold it for ten seconds. Return to center, then slowly twist to the right. Hold ten seconds. Repeat five times. It's important to do this exercise slowly and gently instead of gyrating back and forth like the inside of a washing machine. You don't want to wrench your back before you begin skating.

Neck

Front Head Roll. Stand with feet flat on the floor, eyes forward. Gently drop your chin to your chest, then slowly roll your neck to the right. Stop and hold when your right ear is directly over your shoulder. Hold ten seconds. You'll feel the stretch at the base of your neck. Gently drop your chin to your chest again, then slowly roll your neck to the left, stopping when the left ear is positioned over the left shoulder. Hold ten seconds. It's important *not* to roll the neck backward, as that places an inordinate amount of pressure on the vertebrae of the neck.

Relaxation and stress release are the by-products of a good neck roll. Note: Only roll forward. Never tilt your head back.

Technically, you're now done with the warm-up. Your body is as pliable as Gumby's. For those who want to take it a step further and add strength to that flexibility, let's take a look at the following list of optional exercises to sharpen those skating muscles.

Strengthening

This next set of exercises isn't essential as part of a preskating ritual; you could try them after skating or even first thing in the morning. The purpose is to build up the muscles required of a skater. If you don't do abdominal work or lunges, you'll still be able to roll around the neighborhood just fine, but the strength they will build can only make skating easier.

A good comparison is with downhill skiing. Downhill skiing is a pretty basic sport, with a level of proficiency easily obtained by almost everyone who tries it—just like in-lining. However, skiing requires certain muscles the body isn't used to using. So when skiers drop down the face of a mountain, asking their body to carve sweet S-turns, some are able to keep turning all the way to the bottom without taking a break while others feel a burning in their knees and quadriceps that forces them to take two or three or four breaks before they reach the bottom. Inevitably, they're the folks who tire early and spend the afternoon in the chalet, instead of getting maximum value for their lift ticket by skiing all day.

The same principle is true of in-lining. Granted, there's no such thing as a lift ticket, so whatever value you assign to your skates is of your own doing, but being strong will increase the amount of pleasure you get from in-line skating. Further, you'll find that it will spill over into your everyday life in the form of greater strength and energy. So try these if the mood strikes. They won't make you Arnold Schwarzenegger, but the skating experience will be that much more enjoyable.

Legs

The legs get the full treatment in in-line skating. Buttocks, quadriceps, hamstrings, adductors, abductors, calves, ankles, Achilles tendon—they all contribute to the delicate act of balancing perfectly atop a straight set of narrow, rolling wheels. As such, there are more than a few leg exercises to improve your strength.

Lunges. Stand with hands on hips, feet shoulder-width apart. Begin by taking a giant step forward with your right leg—only instead of following through with the left leg, plant the right foot, so that it is situated 2 to 3 feet in front of the left. Now comes the tricky part. Keeping hands on hips, bend your knees and lower your body until your right quadriceps is parallel with the ground. Raise yourself back up, then step back with the right foot, so that your feet are once again even, still shoulder-width apart. Repeat with the left foot. Alternate each leg fifteen times.

A fun variation is forward lunges. Start the same way, stepping forward with the right foot, only instead of stepping back with the right foot after raising up, keep the right foot planted and step forward with the left. Try going across a room in this manner. Feeling really brave? Try lunging the length of a football field.

Squats. Weight lifters do these with a weighted bar, but they're just as effective without it. Stand with hands on hips, feet shoulder-width apart. Now pretend you're sitting down in an imaginary chair: Thrust your rear end out slightly, bend your knees, and slowly lower your body until the upper (quadriceps) portion of your legs are parallel with the ground. Repeat fifteen times.

Important technique tip: Push up through your heels, instead of rocking forward on your toes. Leaning forward as you push back up puts a great deal of pressure on the lower back.

Toe raises. Stand with hands on hips, feet shoulder-width apart. Lift your heels and stand up on your tippy-toes. Hold for five sec-

The lunge: (1) starting position; (2) step out, shin perpendicular to the ground; (3) lower your body (note that the knee does not touch the ground); (4) return to start.

onds. Lower your heels back to the ground. Repeat fifteen times. To increase the degree of difficulty, grab a thick, hardcover book. Stand atop the book, with your heels on the ground and toes on the book. Raise up to your tiptoes again. Repeat. (Note: To avoid trashing your favorite book, a 2-by-4-inch piece of lumber does the trick just as well.)

Lateral jumps. Place a piece of paper on the floor before you. It doesn't have to be much more than a sheet of typing paper, just big enough that you know it's there. Stand next to and to one side of the paper. Now jump sideways (laterally) so that you land on the other side of the paper. Then jump back. Repeat ten times, then try the same exercise by hopping from leg to leg. In other words, push off with your right leg as you jump over the paper, land on your left, then without putting your right foot down, use your left leg to propel yourself back over the paper.

Abs

Abdominal exercises are ideal for reducing strain on the lower back and supporting the torso as you skate. Remember, although your legs do all the work, balance comes from your center of gravity, which is located somewhere between your belly button and your pubic bone. It's important that this region be strengthened, as it decides what the rest of the body will do as well (amazingly enough, this idea also applies to weight-transfer sports like golf, tennis, skiing, and even baseball).

Crunches. Lie flat on your back with your knees bent and your feet drawn up as close to your rear end as you can bring them. Lace your fingers behind your head. Now, pull yourself up in the manner of a traditional sit-up, but take care to press the lower back into the floor as you lift. Crunches are one of those exercises where the slower you do it, the greater the effect. So lift up slowly (count to four slowly to make sure you get it right) until your shoulder blades are off the floor. Hold at the top. Then slowly lower back down.

If you want to work the lower abdominal region, keep your legs bent, but slide them away from your rear end until they're about two feet away (more or less, depending upon your height). When you lift here, pretend there's a rope situated between your knees and you have to grab ahold of it and pull yourself up. Again, do it slowly, then lower yourself back down.

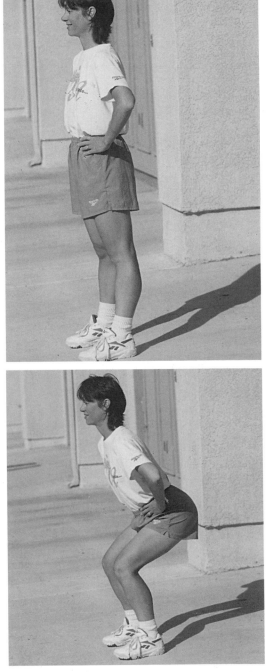

Squats: Start with your back straight, abdominals contracted. Then lower yourself as if you were sitting down in a chair.

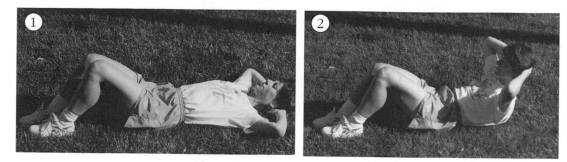

Abdominal crunches: (1) starting position—feet flat, elbows wide; (2) raised position—shoulder blades off the ground, lower back pressed into the ground, chin forward (not touching chest).

Time to Skate

You've stretched and strengthened, warmed up and slipped on your gear. Now it's time to skate. In the interests of honesty, and to give you something to think about as you take those shiny new skates out of the box, let me give you a little preview of how you'll feel a few hours after you get done skating—that is, if your muscles are experiencing skating for the first time.

You'll feel it mostly in your rear end. It's going to feel stiff when you try to stand up from the dinner table tonight. The pain in your quadriceps, abductors, and adductors will be mostly a dull throb as well, so be prepared to exert yourself a little more when standing up or sitting down. Personally, I like these pains. I think they represent honest effort.

Your back might hurt, just because you probably leaned way too far forward (and not the right kind of forward lean—more on this in the chapter on speed skating) as you tried to keep your balance. Your shins and Achilles tendon also may be a bit stiff from learning movements that you've never done before.

Don't despair. This is all part of the toning and strengthening endemic to exercise. Soon you'll be skating without postworkout stiffness, and the sport will feel natural and effortless. Honest.

But first you've got to get out there and do it. So let's go!

5

STRAPPING THEM ON

The Moment You've Been Waiting For

You've waited long enough. It's time to skate. Your muscles are warmed up to the height of elasticity. You've found a section of asphalt free from the teeming masses, a place where you can skate without running into anything and still learn in relative privacy. There is expectation in your legs—the thrill of skating! You try to remember the last time you were on wheels. Was it high school? Before? And then it was on old-fashioned roller skates. What will it feel like to in-line?

Maybe you borrowed a pair of in-line skates recently and had such a great time that you went out and bought your own. Now they lie before you in the box (and in-line boxes are invariably large, impressive arrangements), shiny and new. You spin the wheels once or twice, just to watch them go around. You fiddle with the buckles, making sure that you can thread straps appropriately and cinch the things down around your ankles with a minimum of fuss. Maybe you've stuck your hand inside the inner boot and marveled at how snug everything feels—why, your feet are going to be well taken care of, no doubt about it.

Anticipation, anticipation. Wait no longer. Lift those skates from the box—and I dare you not to feel like a kid on Christmas morning when you do—and feel the heft. Sit down and get ready to put those bad boys on.

Stepping In

Although you carefully read chapter 2 and found the right pair of in-

Taking that first spin around the block.

lines, your feet most likely will not slide right into your skates. There will be, at least for awhile, maybe several weeks, a breaking-in period during which it will be exceedingly difficult to put your skates on. In-line skates are made of molded materials, remember? And molded materials can sometimes be the least pliable substances on the market—until they're broken in. When that day comes, the molded materials begin fitting your foot and ankle like a glove, because you have made them your own. They will move as you move, conform to your contours. So don't despair and imagine that you have extremely large, puffy feet, wholly unsuited to in-line skating if, when you first try to put those skates on, it becomes a battle of wills between you and the boot. You are trying to slip the cumbersome behemoth in place. The boot, suddenly come to life, is resisting your every nuance. The more you tug, the more resistance you encounter. Again, don't despair. That's all part of the new-skate process.

Here are a few tips on making it easier. Examine the boot a moment before putting it on. You'll see an array of buckles, maybe a few laces. The inner boot's tongue will be tucked securely into the backside of the outer boot. (Note: The configuration is not the same for all boots. Just as not all boots have laces or buckles, not all boots have a hard-rubber tongue. Don't panic and think you've bought some sort of substandard skate if you notice yours missing a few items I'm mentioning here.) More than likely, because the boots are new, the actual opening through which you are supposed to slide that sleek, athletic foot of yours is minimal—minimal and inflexible. Help yourself out by taking the following steps:

1. *Unbuckle buckles all the way.* Let the buckle hang freely, so that in no way can it hinder or restrain you while putting your foot in. Take note of how the buckle's pieces slide back together, however. You'll find that a degree in engineering is sometimes necessary to determine which part of the buckle is guided through which opening if you're not observant on the front side.

2. *Untie laces.* Pretend you're slipping on a new pair of high-top sneakers. Remember how tight that can feel? It's impossible to slip on high-tops without loosening the laces for the upper half of the shoe. The same holds for in-lines. You may have to loosen those laces a whole lot farther than you deem appropriate, but remember that these are new skates and that you can always tighten the laces back down once your foot is inside.

It's worth noting that this is not the time to *remove* the laces. If you do so, you will find them next to impossible to rethread after your foot is inside the boot. No, merely loosen for now.

3. *Remove the inner boot.* Think of it as a glove for your foot. Slip that foot-glove out and take a good look at it. Marvel at the mechanics. You may see a piece of elastic connecting the tongue to the remainder of the boot. That is so it doesn't slide around inside the skate when you finally get out on the roads.

   You can do one of two things here. Either slip the inner boot back in, which will give you a greater understanding of how the inner boot connects to the grand scheme of things, or actually slip the inner boot on your foot now, then try to put your now-booted foot back inside the skate. I would caution against the latter. While it works sometimes, it could very well add to your tribulations when the inner boot gets all tangled in that hard-shelled outer boot.

4. *Study the outer boot.* Something akin to Sun-Tzu's reminder to always know your enemy, this is simply the chance for you to study the schematics and plan your method of entry with the least resistance. You'll probably want to slide the tongue out as far as you can to increase foot entry area.

Having said all these things, you may turn out to be one of those lucky few who slide right into your new skates with a minimum of fuss. If so, good for you. For the rest of you, now that buckles and laces are undone, the inner boot is securely anchored, and the outer boot tongue is pulled as far away from the boot as possible, patiently and slowly guide your foot in.

For greater purchase, grab the back of the boot or even the bottom of the wheels and tug. Move your foot every which way until it slides into place. Make sure that your toes can wiggle and that the inner boot didn't get wrinkled or crimped as you put your foot in. If so, take your foot out and fix it without delay. While you may be willing to put up with this nuisance now, it will eventually lead to blisters and an uncomfortable skating experience.

Now that your foot is in place, tighten those laces. Once those are pulled snug and tied, tighten the buckles. As with the buckles of ski boots, always tighten the bottom buckles first and move upward. Once you've cinched the top buckle tight, go back to the bottom and start all over. Why? Because your buckles will loosen as newer adjustments take all the pressure off, creating a situation in which the top buckles will be very tight and the bottom buckles will be extremely loose—unless you retighten.

Proper Way to Put Skate On

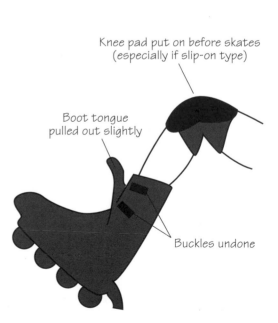

Knee pad put on before skates (especially if slip-on type)

Boot tongue pulled out slightly

Buckles undone

Get Up and Go

When you first rise to your feet, you may feel something like that scene in *Bambi* when he first tries to walk, or the first moments of a colt's life. Perhaps like the first attempts you may have made at ice skating, your knees will be wobbly and knocked, your ankles will probably cave inward, your arms will be akimbo, stuck out perpendicular from your body like a circus performer walking a tightrope. Likewise, when you start to in-line skate, it will be in a skittish, coltish manner. This is why safety gear is so important (as detailed in chapter 3). Now is the time you have the greatest chance of falling before knowing that a fall is upon you. To put that more clearly, you haven't achieved a feel for your skates, so you may not notice when you are suddenly off balance and about to fall until it's too late.

Anyway, look at you: You're on your feet. You've got pads. You've got skates. Now it's time to get moving. Personally, I think the best way to do this is to push away from whatever it is you're balancing against or leaning on or clinging to with all that is within you, and just—go.

A few things to keep in mind:
1. *You're not going to look perfect.* If you do, then you're one of those freaks of nature for whom everything comes naturally and you shouldn't even be reading this book in the first place. For anyone else, you will find yourself rolling with a slightly uncontrollable sensation, trying not to pitch forward (and crash on your face) or backward (elbow dinger). This is OK. It's all part of your body adjusting to life on skates.
2. *You will be acutely aware that you have no clue whatsoever about how to stop.* This is why God invented grass. If you plan your first moments on skates so that a strip of grass is nearby, you merely guide yourself over to the grass and stop. It really works. If there is no grass where you skate, be prepared to skate until you reduce your speed by rolling to a stop or by wrapping your arms around a lamppost—or both.
3. *You hope no one's looking.* But they will be. Big deal. If they're skaters, then they've been through it before and can sympathize. If not, then they're part of that timid group of people dying to try in-lines but afraid they would look, well, like you, on their first day. Either way, you'll move past the awkward, spastic phase quickly and won't have to worry about that.

Be aware, however, that a moment of bravado may overcome you as you notice yourself being watched. In that moment, you will find yourself suddenly comfortable and godlike on skates—a veritable font of skating ability, able to do Brian Boitano's gold-medal Olympic routine all by yourself—and just as suddenly determined to show off your new talents.

Don't. This is when you will crash hardest. You'll be out there trying to impress people, trying to make them think that you are a genuine, bona fide skater. Eventually, you will attempt something that is well beyond your ken, and you will fall. It doesn't just happen to beginners, either. Showing off and its ensuing embarrassment are endemic to all levels of skater. So just be yourself and don't worry that people are watching.

The Basic Push and Glide

Now that you've rolled around uncontrollably for awhile, it's time to begin practicing the fundamentals of real in-line skating. The basic movement we will start with is known as the push and glide. The push and glide is common to both ice-skating and in-line skating, so you have probably seen it done more than a few times. But until you try it, the push and glide can be an illusory sensation. Why? Because it's harder than it looks. Mastering it is the stuff of clinics. But that doesn't mean you should be intimidated. Proficiency in the push and glide is easily attained and is the first step on your road to becoming at home on skates.

Simply, the push and glide is a movement where the lead skate—that is, the skate upon which your weight is centered and which skates in a forward motion—is the beneficiary of the efforts of the pushing skate—that is, the "glide." Obviously, each skate alternates as lead skate and pushing skate. The idea is to center your weight so perfectly atop the lead skate that it moves effortlessly (and without wobbling) while the pushing skate pushes slightly laterally and to the rear of the body.

If it sounds complicated, it's because it can be. But like anything, when broken down into increments, it can be simple. In fact, you have probably already begun pushing and gliding in your first few moments on skates without knowing it. Unless you just rolled aimlessly, I can almost guarantee that you spent a few seconds pushing and gliding, as this is the most natural method of controlling direction and speed on in-lines.

Push and Glide Diagram

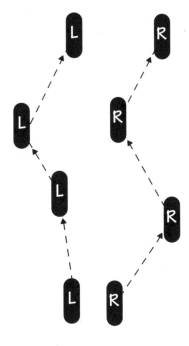

Relaxation and Visualization

Before we try a few exercises to increase push-and-glide profi-ciency, take a few more minutes and skate around. Notice what you're doing. Chances are, one leg is pointing in the direction you wish to travel while the other leg is providing the locomotion to get there. Without thinking about it too much (as this is where natural movement most always gets stilted in favor of those awkward, re-hearsed movements that inhibit natural movement), consciously push and glide around your practice area. Push with one leg, lead with the other. Push with one leg, lead with the other.

Feel it? What you're doing is the same movement people have performed for centuries on ice skates, and more recently on roller skates and in-lines. Try it again, this time visualizing yourself as an Olympic figure skater or hockey player. Think of their bold pushing movements and long, effortless glides. Feel yourself lengthening your own push stroke and holding that glide just a few seconds more. Visualize again. This time imagine yourself skating directly *be-hind* that same elite skater. Imagine that you are copying that skater's movements. Push, boldly and with enough power to propel you forward appropriately and in control. Glide, not worrying about balance, but focusing on staying atop the glide long enough to get maximum benefit. (One big problem new skaters have is that they get skittish atop the glide. Afraid they'll fall, new skaters often stop gliding before they run out of momentum and resort to a short, choppy skating technique. Needless to say, this is very inefficient.)

Note: It's impossible to overemphasize the importance of the re-laxation that must accompany this visualization. Remember that re-laxed muscles are more likely to be responsive and hold the body less rigid. Relaxed muscles aren't thinking of crashing, they're look-ing ahead with anticipation to the thrill of skating. That's why relax-ation is so important when it comes to visualization, because your brain's first impulse is self-preservation. The brain will override (or try to) the impulse to relax and skate along with the visualization. Your brain will remind you again and again that you are a novice and that foolishly imagining yourself skating along behind top skaters can only lead to calamity. In the process, your brain—if you listen to it—will cause your muscles to grow tense. The next step? You *will* fall.

Ignore your brain. Relax. Keep those muscles loose and try to ig-nore those self-preservatory thoughts (not all of them, though; re-member, there are cars out there). Focus instead on visualization and relaxation. In-line skating is not life and death. Even if it were, relaxation would still be crucial.

The Movements

Back to skating. Broken down into their most elemental phases, pushing and gliding are two distinct movements. The glide is the act of centering the weight perfectly over the center of the skate's wheel, neither to one side nor the other, for as long as possible. The push is the act of driving the rear leg away from the body in a single smooth motion that sees the inside portion of the wheels grip the ground for a brief second, then uses that resistance to push away. This movement is done in a lateral-behind direction. Sounds confusing, but if you can imagine yourself on a map, skating due north, the push motion would occur in a southeasterly direction.

After pushing off, the rear leg steps forward and places itself quietly on the ground, ready to assume the role of glide leg. It goes something like this: Push, move the rear leg forward, place it softly on the ground in preparation of a glide, then push off again, this time with the other leg. If it sounds confusing, it's because it can be. That's why it's so important to relax and *do* instead of preoccupying yourself with thinking too much. Your body will know what to do if you just let it.

Push-and-Glide Drills

Now let's try a few drills.

One-legged drills. This is not skating on one leg. That part will come soon enough. Rather, this is teaching your body to push and glide by teaching one leg at a time. Start with your left leg as the lead leg. Push off with your right. Feel the muscles of the shin, ankle, and calf of the left leg tense slightly to support the glide. Hold that glide as long as possible. Now, instead of pushing off with the left leg like you normally would, push off with the right again. And again and again and again. Repeat this ten times, then switch legs so that your right leg is lead leg and the left is doing all the work.

Glide. A variation on the one-legged drill, this drill exaggerates the glide movement in order to teach when the glide is too long or too short. Start with your left leg again. Push off powerfully with your right. Now glide on that left leg again for as long as you possibly can. Again, the idea is to exaggerate the glide, so if you can hold it until you totally run out of momentum and are on the verge of toppling over, all the better. As soon as you get to the point where

Proper Glide Alignment

(Note: On improper glide, wheel is bent inward or outward, depending which way ankle is turned.)

you feel uncomfortable, push off with the right leg again. Repeat this ten times, then switch legs.

Push. The reverse of the glide drill, this exercise teaches the dynamics of pushing. Start with the left leg again. Push off, glide, but push off again and again and again, each time well before the glide has reached its zenith. The point is to emphasize the power of the pushing motion. Remember, in the push phase, the quadriceps and gluteus muscles are like a piston driving the skate away from the body (think "southeast") to power the glide skate forward.

Double Push. This almost doubles as a conditioning exercise because it's so tough on the muscles of the lower body. Start with the left leg. Push off with the right. Now, instead of emphasizing the glide, push off quickly with the right leg. Repeat this several times, making sure to focus on pushing instead of gliding. What you will notice (other than the fact that your quads and rear are on fire from the concentrated effort) is that the dynamics of pushing off have become second nature and are slowly working their way into that complicated firing of muscle neurons known as "muscle memory."

Putting it together. Now go back to your normal skating. Push off smoothly and let the glide go on optimally. Feel the glide end just as

Proper Angle of Pushing Skate

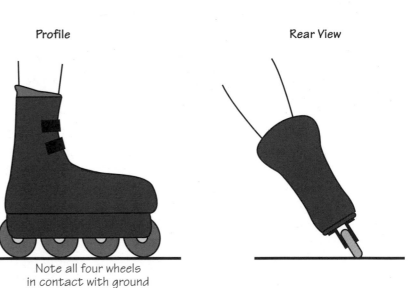

Profile

Rear View

Note all four wheels
in contact with ground

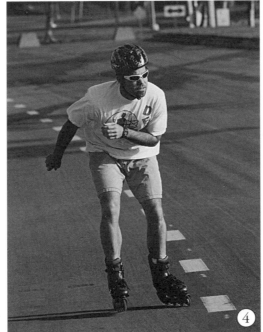

Proper form for the push and glide: relaxation, slight forward lean, loose arms, head up. Note the weight distributed evenly over the wheels in photo 1 to ensure optimum glide. Also, note that all four wheels are touching the ground during the "push" phase to achieve maximum propulsion.

How not to focus your center of gravity: (1) weight too far forward (skater is bending at the hips); (2) weight too far back (no bend at the hips or knees).

the rear leg moves up to position itself for the glide and the lead leg positions itself to become the pushing leg. It's very complicated on paper, needlessly so. Simply do it, and you'll feel what I'm talking about.

Center of Gravity

The crucial intangible as all this push and glide becomes second nature is balance. It's what makes the glide so difficult and the reason your pushes can be less than wholehearted affairs. Call it fear of falling, but another spin might be that you are feeling absolutely clueless about how to control your balance. Until you can control your balance, you will have a very hard time achieving success at in-line skating.

Ever watch a wide receiver make a twisting, seemingly impossible midair catch—the kind where his body is so far out of whack that you wonder how in the world he could land without killing himself, let alone catch a football? Well, the reason he caught that ball has everything to do with him being aware of his center of gravity and how it relates to balance. If you can capture a greater awareness of your center of gravity, you will find in-lining a whole lot easier. In turn, it will help your ability to do everything from hit a golf ball or tennis ball to hike along a mountain trail. Balance is everything.

Where is your center of gravity? Somewhere between your belly button and your pubic bone. It varies from individual to individual. Where it is, though, is not as important as how you relate to it.

When most people are learning to in-line skate, they forget all about the center of gravity and try to balance atop their skates using just their legs. In effect, the legs—probably somewhere in either the shins or the quadriceps—become the focus of balance. People who do this find themselves skating like someone on stilts, always swaying forward and back to control their movements. Similarly, some individuals go through a "top-heavy" phase when learning to skate. They figure that their balance lies somewhere in the head and shoulders, maybe the arms. They figure that if they flail enough and hunch their shoulders at just the right angle, they can prevent a fall—which, of course, doesn't work.

The proper technique, which people get around to if they skate for more than just a day or two, is to let your lower torso—the area from the top of your hips to your belly button—control your movements. If you can imagine this area as the fulcrum around which the

Proper Recreational Form

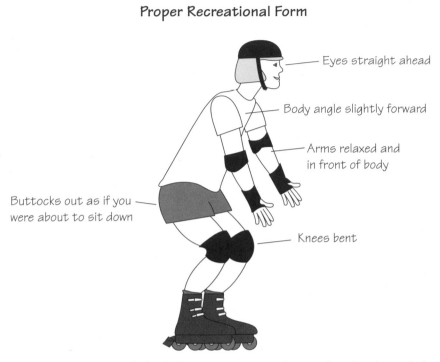

Eyes straight ahead

Body angle slightly forward

Arms relaxed and in front of body

Buttocks out as if you were about to sit down

Knees bent

Ahh ... relaxation—and a nice, low center of gravity

body pivots you will find the urge to sway forward or backward disappearing. The shoulder movement goes away as the upper body learns the meaning of "quiet."

How to make this technique work for you? First, that rear end of yours—the one that wants to prop your body upright by tucking directly under your rib cage—stick it out a bit in back. I'll say this again and again, but pretend that you're about to sit in a chair. It's a little-known fact, but when you are about to sit in a chair, your weight is balanced perfectly from the time you begin lowering yourself until the time you come to rest. If not, you find yourself landing in the chair with one of those mighty plops associated with fatigue.

So stick that butt out. Don't be shy. Now, visualize again that great skater you were skating behind earlier. Think about how his or her body flowed up and down the ice. Notice anything? Other than perfection, what you saw were hips and lower torso almost entirely devoid of superfluous movement. Too often people think that in-lining means accentuating each push and glide with a hip thrust or shimmy. In fact, the opposite is true. When your center of gravity is controlling your movements, every movement radiates outward while the center of gravity stays relatively immobile.

Diagram of a
Snowplow Stop

Stopping

I put this section toward the end of the chapter instead of at the beginning because I want you to focus more on forward movement—the act of going—than on the act of stopping that movement. Let's face it, as a new skater, the first thing you think of once you get up a good head of steam is how to stop, to the detraction of all else. And by now, if you have been doing the drills and practicing your center-of-gravity technique, you're developing a pretty solid grasp of how to stop without killing yourself—even if that means stepping on the grass. But let's define and refine the act of stopping, so that it seems less a random act of survival than a purposeful method of controlling the skates instead of the skates controlling you.

The easiest way for a new skater to learn to stop is also the easiest way for a new skier. It's called the *snowplow,* and basically it involves pointing your knees and the toes of both skates inward as you roll, thus reducing forward movement. It's a great technique, but not the most aesthetic.

The Heel Brake

But there's more. So now let's talk about the heel brake. You know where it is. It's right there behind your heel, and if you grew up on regular roller skates, where the brake is in front of the toe, you are probably wondering how in the world to use that heel brake without killing yourself.

If I can place an aside in here, I've always wondered why it is that people are more afraid of heel brakes than toe brakes. Personally, if I'm going to fall, I would rather fall backwards—where I'm better padded, with the special padding on my elbows and natural padding on my derriere—than forward, where my relatively poorly padded palms and those fragile carpal bones in my wrists are the only thing preventing my face from taking a beating.

That said, the heel brake is a simple piece of work. Its use involves sliding one foot slightly in front of the other, bending the rear leg, and rocking back onto the rear heel to let the brake drag the ground. Place more pressure on it as you feel speed drain away, until you finally come to a stop.

Let's go through that again, but this time pretend that you're skating toward a brick wall. Extend one foot slightly in front of the other. This provides balance for what you are about to do. Next, with that wall getting closer and your fear at an all-time high, bend the rear leg at the knee. This is not a "down to the ground" curtsy we're talking

Using a Heel Brake

Move foot with brake
ahead of the other foot

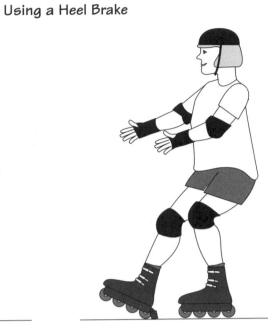

Lift toes and gently apply
pressure with brake

Stopping Against a Wall

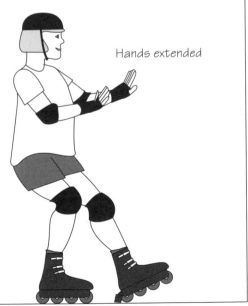

Hands extended

Heel brake in use

Using heel brake. Notice bent knees.

Diagram of Drag Braking
(T-Stop)

Profile of Drag Braking
(T-Stop)

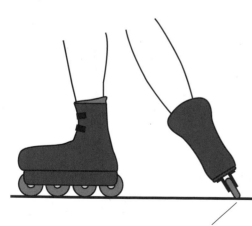

Friction applied here

about, merely a slight depression of the rear knee to put the rear skate in position for what you are about to do next, which is lift the toe of the forward skate so that the heel brake drags lightly on the ground. As you begin to slow down and get closer to the wall, close enough to admire the masonry, put more pressure on the heel brake until you come to a complete stop. Whew! You made it.

It's important to note that use of the heel brake is not performed during a push-and-glide phase. When you see a potential stop situation coming, cease the push and glide and coast in an upright position with both legs parallel. Brake from that position; or, if you decide not to stop, coast in that fashion until the urge to stop passes, then resume pushing and gliding.

Other Stopping Methods

A neat trick to reduce speed without using the heel brake is to drag the front wheels of one skate behind the other. Some call this a T-stop. It involves crossing the rear leg over slightly and being able to glide on one leg while dragging the wheels of the other skate. Needless to say, it's a more delicate balancing trick than the regular heel brake technique. Try it, though, when you get a little more comfortable as a skater. It's a great technique for slowing down. It also looks pretty cool.

Another method of stopping, once you've developed a feel for making subtle turns, is the turn stop. Slowly arc in lazy turns that will trim speed without requiring the brakes. This method is very popular among in-line hockey players. Avoid, however, the traditional "hockey stop," which is an ice-only method of stopping that involves turning both skates abruptly in a parallel fashion. While impressive on the ice, it's a prescription for injury on pavement. Only the very best skaters should try it.

Turning

Let's review what we have covered so far in this chapter: starting, skating, stopping. All pretty fundamental stuff, so maybe it's time we add a little spice like, say, a turn. While not the most radical of maneuvers, a turn can feel downright treacherous the first time you try one. Your feet will splay, your arms will swing out wide to keep you from falling, and you will most likely barely make it thorough the turn. In short, an improper turn can become an exercise in how *not* to balance.

You could instead execute the entire turn with both skates parallel and directly beneath your hips and shoulders. Sure, you would complete the turn, but without the sort of panache one expects from a skating genius. You'd look like you're anchored inside a full-body cast as you make the turn. It's a stiff, clunky way to go about turning, and it's not at all aesthetic. Worse, it will hinder your growth as a skater by teaching you poor habits.

How to turn properly? To find out, let's go through the basics of turning. Again, this is a situation where relaxation is key. If you can convince yourself to be rid of that fear of falling that fills you with so much tension, I guarantee that learning to turn will be much easier.

Basic Turns

Begin by getting up a good head of steam. (You don't want to go too fast into your first turns, a sure calamity, but you don't want to dodder in so slowly that you lose the momentum that makes turning easier.) Let's say that you are going to make a right turn around an orange traffic cone that you've placed in the middle of the local playground (playgrounds—*empty* playgrounds—are the best places to practice). Skating toward the cone—knees slightly bent, center of gravity over your skates, skates shoulder-width apart, body relaxed—begin your turn 10 to 15 feet in front of the cone. Slide the inner, or right, skate *slightly* in front of the left—not a foot or two in front, just enough that the heel of the right skate is roughly parallel with or behind the toe of the left. Now, lean slightly, so that the inside edge of your wheels is carrying your weight instead of the center. Be careful to keep your center of gravity solid. Keeping the skates in position, and watching the weight over that inside wheel, slowly carve your turn. Believe it or not, if you stay cognizant of your balance, it should be a fairly easy process.

Having said all that, here are a few trouble spots to watch out for.
1. *You are afraid to slip your right foot in front of your left.* Let's face it, it's an act of faith. When you're new to skates, any sort of balance is precarious and precious. The thought of tampering with that balance can seem an act of heresy. Two words of advice: Don't worry. Slipping your right foot 6 inches in front of the left (or vice versa for a left turn) will not cause you to crash—if you keep your balance properly weighted.
2. *Improper weight distribution.* Sometimes people start to take a right turn by sliding the right skate forward, but then make the mistake of placing *all* their weight on that skate. That leads to either an off-balance turn, where the inside leg guides the body

single-handedly, or a crash. Remember, distribute your weight evenly between both skates. The inside skate is to be a guide, nothing more. The reason for sliding the inside foot slightly forward is to reduce the turning arc, not to absorb all the weight.

3. *You could tangle both skates.* There are a number of ways to accomplish this, none of which have aesthetic potential. Avoid tangling your skates at all costs.

Crossover Turns

Whenever I think of crossover turns, I think of Olympic speed skaters powering through a corner, body slung so low that their fingertips almost brush the ice for balance, legs driving like pistons, eyes facing far down the track. It is perhaps the most aesthetically pleasing and functional turn in existence. It is also not as difficult as it looks. However, before attempting a crossover, it's important that you be adept at turning fundamentals and are comfortable weighting and unweighting through a turn. It also helps to have a keen awareness of each skate's location in reference to the other, as the greatest hazard involved in crossovers is getting skates tangled up in each other.

Begin by aiming toward that same orange cone you turned around a few minutes ago. Come into it easily, maybe a little more slowly than during normal turns. The reason is that it's important to get your body used to doing a crossover at slow speeds. The slower speed allows plenty of reaction time in case of a miscue. It also allows you to focus more on what your skates are doing than the actual act of turning.

Let me explain. A crossover is a series of powerful, alternating strokes. Each leg is off the ground (and in the process of crossing over in front of the other) while the other is simultaneously edging through the turn and driving forward. It's the sort of maneuver that takes a bit of initial thought.

So let's go back to that cone again, making another right turn. Begin the turn like any other, with the right foot sliding slightly forward and your weight shifting to the inside edge of the wheels. Only now, instead of keeping the left foot static, lift it off the ground and *cross it over* well in front of the right. Once the left skate plants firmly on pavement, lift the right foot off the ground. Now the left skate is defining the turn, while the right foot is preparing to cross over the left and take its turn as the defining skate.

See what's going on here? Each skate is basically performing a

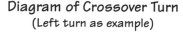

Diagram of Crossover Turn
(Left turn as example)

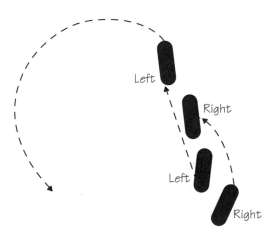

The crossover. Concentration and relaxation make for a dynamic, speed-building turn.

push and glide. This is the reason that crossovers can be such a great source of powering through turns. For, unlike regular turns, which siphon off speed (and are even a recognized form of braking), crossovers actually increase speed with each stroke. The secret is in planting each skate with deliberation—which occurs naturally when that skate defined the arc of the turn—and pushing off with equal deliberation. Again, this occurs naturally to propel one skate over the top of the other.

One thing to watch out for is to use both legs evenly when pushing through a turn. To maximize speed it's important that one leg is not doing more work than another. The reason many people fail to use both skates evenly has to do with a fear that they have less control on one leg or the other. For instance, I'm right-handed, and my right leg is the leg I favor when I skate. As such, I am not as comfortable with balancing on my left leg as I am with balancing on my right. When I power through a crossover, I have to consciously push with equal strength with both legs. I won't crash if I fail to do so, but my potential for maximizing speed is vastly reduced.

Most skaters, I know from experience, favor one leg over the other. If that applies to you, don't be discouraged. A good confidence-building drill is all that is required to fix the problem. Try this: When performing a crossover, exaggerate the amount of time you spend on your weaker skate. Do so by lifting the other leg extremely—absurdly—high when crossing over. This will force you to either learn to balance comfortably on that weaker skate—or crash. That won't happen, of course, because you are a confident, relaxed skater. Focus on the drill instead of on your fear of falling, and the crossover will become a valued part of your ability arsenal.

Preventing a Fall

Instead of discussing how to fall, which is a tough activity to control—you will rarely be able to anticipate the moment when you will splat hard against either the ground or some immobile object—I think it's better to imagine how to prepare for a fall. In a word: prevention. Always skate with a preventative frame of mind. No, you won't be able to prevent that nasty fall, but you will be able to prevent the aftereffects by relaxing as you skate.

Keep your body loose at all times: knees bent, arms loosely to the sides, center of gravity low. This puts your body in a position to absorb a fall that much better. A stiff body feels much more pain than a relaxed one. A good example, although not pertaining directly to in-lining: A few years ago while I was riding my bike, a courier abruptly pulled his car into the bike lane before me—I mean, right before me. Being a courier, he immediately opened his door to race inside whatever building he was visiting, so after I somehow managed to successfully swerve around his suddenly parked vehicle, the added obstacle of an opening door and an emerging body were added to the mix. I swerved again, but not enough to miss the door entirely. My front wheel caught on it, and I was launched from my bike. But because I'd had so little time to prepare for the crash—everything, from parking to opening the door to crash, happened within a second—and because I'd already been relaxed from cruising along on my bike, I miraculously managed to land like a rag doll, then roll. My bike was totaled, but I had no aftereffects other than a massive adrenaline rush that made my knees almost buckle.

The same principle for prevention applies to in-lining. Stay relaxed, stay loose. Your body will absorb the crash a lot easier if you're a rag doll than if you're frozen in place.

Brave New Worlds

It's time to take those hotshot new skating skills off the local playground or empty parking lot and put them to use in the real world. You know how to stop and start and turn. You have a fair sense of balance. You can prevent a fall. The only thing standing between you and exploring a broader world of in-lining is yourself.

So where to go first?

Around the block. Take a spin around your neighborhood. Even if you've lived there all your life, you will most definitely see it as you've never seen it before. You'll notice where the pavement is smooth and true, laid with care and patience by workers who were not hustling to break for lunch, and where the pavement is uneven and cracked, filled with potholes. These will present wondrous obstacles that you never knew existed.

You will notice which turns are off-camber, which are not. You'll see where the sidewalk is level and also where that big oak tree's roots grew underneath to lift the concrete into earthquakelike tilts. But most of all, you'll make a pretty quick decision whether or not your block is the type of place you would deem appropriate to your growth as a skater.

The bike path. Smooth, winding, seemingly filled with a sense of

Cruising on in-line skates lets you see the neighborhood as you never have before.

destination, the local bike path is a great place to in-line skate. Just one problem: It was designed for cyclists, so there are a couple of key rules to follow. First, stay to the far right side of the trail. Cyclists go faster than skaters, so if you stay to the left or in the center, passing will be a true chore for them and could lead to a crash if you and they get tangled. Second, don't skate abreast, for the same reason.

Hills. Maybe it's a little early to be talking about hills, but you're going to run into them sooner or later, so it's best to be prepared. They can be great fun if handled properly, but there's no greater sense of panic than that which an out-of-control in-line skater feels going downhill. A few rules to follow if you do try hills:

1. *Start off with gentle inclines.* Make that *short,* gentle inclines. You need to learn the feel of speed beneath your wheels. Once you adjust to this sensation on short hills, feel free to graduate to something bigger.

2. *Learn to make S-turns to check your speed.* Think of slalom skiers going down a mountain. If they were to go straight down, they would go much faster. But through the use of strategic turns, the speed is drained enough to keep it under control. Whether through sweeping turns that encompass a huge arc, or simply short, tight turns, know that the S-turn is your friend. Stay relaxed. Keep your weight centered and your feet a shoulder-width apart.

3. *Always have a bailout plan.* This may be a grassy stretch along side the road, or it may be an intersecting road that gently curves uphill that can be used as a runoff ramp. Whatever. Once you lose control of your speed, it's extremely hard to get it back, and road rash is a very painful matter. So think ahead and have a plan for avoiding calamity.

You're ready for more. You've gone from novice to neighborhood cruiser. In the next chapter we'll discuss a few moves that will fine-tune your skating abilities and increase your confidence level. We'll also look at a few techniques to prepare you for such in-line niches as in-line hockey, extreme skating, or speed skating.

Oh, and one more time: Relax.

6

UPPING THE ANTE

Beyond the Basics

By now you've achieved a level of proficiency with your skating. It's no longer awkward to slip into your skates and roll around the block. The concept of turning, in all its vagaries and complexities, is not something to be feared. You even feel comfortable calling yourself an in-line skater in front of your friends, sure that you can back it up.

Now it's time to stake the step from beginning skater to intermediate. It's a necessary passage, as the fundamental skills you've learned so far have provided the building blocks that will allow you to experience such in-line joy as hockey, extreme skating, and speed skating, but have not been refined enough to allow you to perform the technical machinations required of these aspects of in-lining.

What am I talking about here? Well, skating backward, for instance. Hockey players cannot play effective defense or play a full, dynamic game until they learn that skating backward is just as necessary as skating forward. In extreme skating, such moves as a *fakie,* in which the skater goes down a ramp backward, demand even more that an individual be able to skate backward. In speed skating, of course, skating backward is not necessary—I can say with certainty that there are no backward races in existence—but the ability to skate backward will help if you must dodge a crash, then find yourself spun around into the sort of off-balance position that a coupe of backward strokes might alleviate.

I'm also talking about slaloming. We touched briefly on it in the previous chapter as a method of siphoning off speed, but now we will go a step further. While the weaving motion of slalom skating obviously benefits in-line hockey players, it will benefit the average

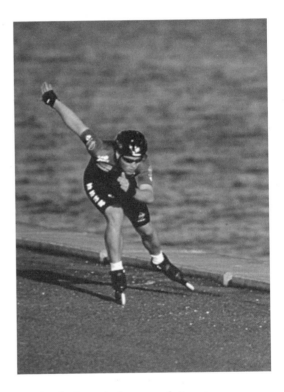

Moving farther out of your comfort zone.

skater, too. Imagine a trip around the block or down to the grocery store. Somewhere along that trek, there will be obstacles—maybe a child on a bicycle, maybe a handful of pebbles that someone scattered on the pavement—that must be avoid quickly. To do that, you must be able to slalom effectively.

These are just a few of the reasons that I urge you to push yourself past the beginner phase. It will be difficult at first, just as your very first day on skates was, because the process of trying something newer and more challenging involves the physical and mental effort of leaving your comfort zone. The alternative is to maintain the level of skating prowess you have already acquired and to push yourself no further. However, it's my feeling that such a move would lead to a feeling of unfinished business with your skating. This is not to advocate a lifestyle of full-fledged commitment to your skates, spending every waking hour fine-tuning your bearings and polishing the polyethylene shell, poring over skate magazines and catalogs. Such behavior is obsessive and ultimately counterproductive to the idea that skating is a method of improving your quality of life.

No, what I mean by pushing yourself out of the comfort zone is the physical act of trying new things just for the sake of trying them, aware constantly that you will fail several times before achieving proficiency. But you will achieve it. And in a sense, it will be harder to accept the fact that you will struggle to make this leap than it was to accept the falls and miscues of your first day on skates. Why? Because you think of yourself as a skater now. In that capacity, you probably stopped looking foolish on skates some time ago. The idea that you could revisit some of that foolishness now, just for the sake of learning aesthetics, may be hard to accept.

But try, because once you make the leap beyond beginner, the whole of skating will begin to unfold before you. There will be things that you will be able to do on skates that you never thought possible—and after awhile they will seem impossibly easy.

Where to Start

Begin by changing your mind-set. No longer are you a beginner, struggling to roll down the driveway without impaling yourself on the neighbors' rosebushes. Now you should think of yourself as being a step above. This is not meant to be an elitist emotion but, rather, a way of thinking of yourself and your skating. It's an imagery thing. When you think well of yourself, you become better. If you still think of yourself as a beginner, then you will remain a beginner—in your own eyes. Think of yourself as intermediate or better, and you will notice a quiet confidence in your skating. You may find yourself skating with a better posture, even helping others with minute adjustments. This is all part of the mind-set you should have as you begin attempting a few new moves.

Skating Backward

When I was a kid, the best way to skate was on roller skates and the best *place* to skate was the local roller rink. Those of you with similar experience will know what I'm talking about—Saturday afternoon, renting a pair of lace-ups, stepping onto that supersmooth floor, and skating for hours in a clockwise direction. I was something of a terror, more concerned with speed than anything else, but the one group of people I invariably envied were those who could skate backward. There were two reasons for my hidden jealousy. First, I could not skate backward, because my passion for speed never allowed time to learn the nuances of going backward (like I said before, there are no races in a backward direction). Second, they made it look so easy. How, I wondered, could anyone make the act of skating in without knowing where you were going look so simple? The answer: It's not as tough as it looks.

The Hourglass

Unlike the normal push and glide, skating backward using the "hourglass" technique is more about moving the legs in a tandem sculling motion. The idea is to begin with both feet parallel, shoulder-width apart, then simultaneously move the rear of both skates away from each other (not much more than 6 inches), then slowly bring them back to a position parallel and shoulder-width apart. It sounds difficult, but it's really not. The biggest difficulty in learning this move is watching that your wheels move inward and outward in a continuous arc instead of a series of herky-jerky motions. Also, your balance will feel impaired, because your tendency will be to lean forward—away from the direction you're going.

Let's go through this technique again. First, begin in a wide-open area. It's more important now than ever that there be few, if any, obstacles on the skating surface. Again, playgrounds work great (if they're empty). After warming up and double-checking your pads (elbow pads being more important than knee pads; helmet being more important than ever), stop and place your feet parallel to each

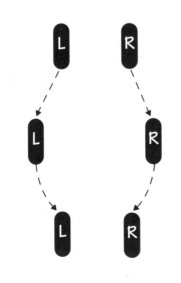

Diagram of Skating Backward
(Hourglass)

other, shoulder-width apart, on the pavement. This is where it gets tricky. You need a bit of locomotion to facilitate the turning process, so either push away from something like a wall or have a skating partner give you a gentle backward push. Remember to keep your feet parallel as you begin.

Now, slowly spread your heels away from each other by placing weight on the inner edge of your wheels (both sets). This should be a gradual movement, not something that occurs in a staccato motion. A good way to tell when you have moved your heels far enough away from each other is to spread your arms. If your heels are elbow-width apart, then you have gone far enough.

When you go to move your heels back together, resist the urge to lift your feet off the ground. Instead, make sure to keep that weight over the inner edge of both wheels (this is what makes the heels go in and out) and slowly groove the heels back together. Once you've done that, your heels should be facing straight backward. This is the coasting position. Just as in the push and glide, you want to maximize the coast time. Cut it too short and you lose the momentum you build with each hourglass heel movement, which you will repeat again and again to continue the backward movement. Again, it sounds tough, but it's easy with a bit of practice. Points to remember are keeping the weight over the inner wheel edges and not letting your skates come up off the ground as you make the hourglass movement.

After you achieve a level of proficiency, it will no longer be necessary to have a friend or handy wall help you get started. The hourglass movement will become much simpler and second nature, and you'll know how to use it to start from a still position.

A Tip on Balance. Ironically enough, it's important to keep the same balance position when facing forward and backward. You remember it: torso slightly bent at the waist, knees bent. The only change you'll make is to have your arms slightly thrown back (again, the elbows are a point of reference: keep them pointed, like you're imitating a chicken or Mick Jagger) and to turn your head slightly to watch where you're going.

Reverse Push and Glide

Whereas the hourglass is a smooth inward and outward movement of the heels, skates never leaving the ground, the reverse push and glide is a conscious lifting of the skates to facilitate backward movement. This may seem a more logical method of backward skat-

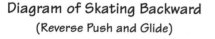

Diagram of Skating Backward
(Reverse Push and Glide)

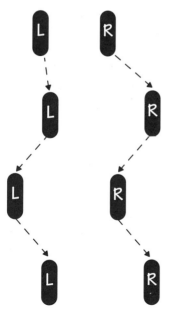

Skating backward. Note that the weight is positioned neither too far forward nor too far back. Also, the skater constantly glances over his shoulder to get bearings.

ing—and in many ways it is—but it is also fraught with a touch more peril, which is why it is more difficult than the hourglass.

The motion is a simple reversal of the basic push and glide (described in detail in chapter 5). One skate pushes off while the other charts direction and bears the weight over the center of the wheels. The problem comes about when skaters either forget to lean forward enough to offset the backward motion or let the glide skate get out of control and do the kind of wacky things that an out-of-control skate can do—things that throw the body off balance and make the legs splay and catch on the pavement, causing a crash.

There are a number of ways to prevent such occurrences, but let's begin by walking through the technique first. As with the hourglass, start by leaning against a stationary object, something that will give you a sense of security before trying something new. Now, after pushing off slightly, you want to let one skate—let's say the right—push slightly away and forward of your body. This is not a sweeping, exaggerated leg propulsion as in a normal push and glide, but more an outward flick that creates a balanced sense of movement. After pushing off, return that right leg to a position parallel to the left, so that you are rolling backward with both feet charting your direction. The next time you push off, it will be with the left foot. Again, return it to the parallel position so that you might roll backward in control.

In a nutshell, that's how you do it. Once this movement becomes second nature and you feel comfortable going faster, you can increase speed by leaving out the parallel glide and simply glide on one skate at a time. In this manner you will constantly increase speed, so be careful that you don't get out of control and smack your head. (Remember, the chance for head injury is greater in backward skating because the rear of the head is the first thing that hits the ground in a fall. Please wear your helmet.) Also, remember to look back for objects that might get in the way.

The two trouble spots we discussed earlier can be alleviated simply. First, to prevent those nasty backward spills, make sure to maintain the same forward lean as in a forward push and glide: Knees bent, weight focused on the center of gravity instead of the upper body or legs. Second, and more important, to prevent the glide skate from squirreling out of control, use the muscles in the foot, ankle, and shin to keep the wheels rolling in a straight line. Beware of rolling your ankle outward or inward so that the skate is rolling on the corresponding outer or inner wheel edges. That is where your skates will get away from you, turning without your wanting them to. Always use the center of the wheels, which gives you the greatest amount of control and balance. If it helps make this task easier, skate with your feet slightly farther apart than shoulder width, which will make balance easier and allow you to focus on wheel placement instead of falling down.

Turning Around

The alternative to starting your backward skate from a motionless position is to switch directions on the fly. This, unlike plain old backward skating, *is* as hard as it looks. The movement can flummox even experienced skaters if the tricky weight transfer is not done properly. However, this is one move that's well worth learning, if only for the versatility it will bring to your skating arsenal.

If there's any solace, the turnaround movement is simple to visualize. It's the simple act of switching from the push and glide (more precisely, the turn happens during the glide portion) to a backward motion. The turn is quick, as befits something that involves shifting from a rapid forward to backward movement without falling.

Begin by skating slowly, pushing and gliding lightly. Get into a

Diagram of Turning Around

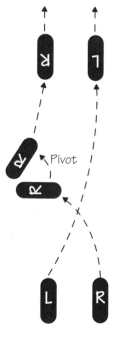

Turning around: It's all in the pivot (photo 2).

rhythm, making sure to fully extend the glide. To execute the turnaround properly, it must take place in that split second during the push and glide when neither skate is fully weighted. Let's say that you are gliding on your left leg and you have pushed off with your right. As you begin to lose momentum on the glide, pivot on the toe of the left leg so that your torso swings around from a forward to backward angle. You should finish the pivot with both feet traveling in a backward motion, parallel, shoulder-width apart. From here you can resume the normal reverse push and glide.

The sticky point, of course, is the pivot. It is a minor pirouette, not some great balletic leap. It is merely meant to change your direction. Don't feel compelled to soar to Baryshnikovian heights while pivoting; merely unweight the front toe of the glide foot slightly and pivot on it. Remember to bend at the knees and spring slightly from the bend to help you execute the turnaround.

Power Strokes

The epitome of recreational in-line skating are those individuals who make it look effortless while zooming down a stretch of pavement at Mach speed. Though not speed skaters, they skate bent double, windmilling the arms to increase speed and balance. They use four-

Taking the push and glide to new frontiers.

wheeled skates, unlike speed skaters, so their ability to control these potentially horrific speeds is further cause for applause. They can invariably stop on a dime. In short, they look as if they were born on skates.

That's not the case, of course. They have simply managed to elevate their skating ability by practice, practice, practice. Their push and glide has been refined to a thing of beauty, with each stroke pushing them and gliding them farther than any beginning skater's similar strokes. That's what makes these almost surreal skaters so spectacular. Their ability to seemingly hover above the pavement is what we all strive for, but so rarely achieve.

What they are doing, for lack of a better term, are *power strokes.* Their robust, fluid skating style is a combination of the basic push and glide and the speed skater's racing aura. Amazingly, learning this technique is not a matter of learning something new and potentially difficult, as in doing a turnaround. Power strokes are simply a thorough refinement of the basic push and glide, but with the addition of power and explosiveness.

Let's begin by reexamining the push and glide. Think back. Depending on how quickly you have picked up skating, those first few moments with the push and glide could be weeks or months behind you. Remember that the desire is to continue the glide until you have reached that gray area somewhere between where your speed peaks and momentum begins to ebb. Remember that the push should be a single solid sweep away from the body (think "southwest") that propels you forward.

Practice each of those moves a few times again. (I like to think of that old saying: Practice doesn't make perfect; perfect practice makes perfect.) Exaggerate both the push and the glide to sear into your brain how they feel when done perfectly. Feel how that pushing leg drives your leg away from your body? Feel how your shin, ankle, and foot muscles work in harmony to keep the weight of your feet directly over the center of your wheels? Feel how your body is crouched, poised, relaxed?

Building on the Push and Glide

Now let's try an exercise that builds on those sensations, starting with the "push" phase. Before beginning, it's worth pointing out that the power in your push stroke comes from your gluteus (buttock), quadricep (front portion of your thigh), and adductor and abductor (inner and outer thigh) muscles. This set of muscles is the heart of in-line skating, the power plant. Think of this region of your body as the locomotive driving the in-line engine. During a power stroke the idea is to turbocharge that locomotive. You want that push stroke of yours to give you extra speed, extra power. You want the push stroke to drive you farther and faster than you ever thought possible.

The power stroke is accomplished by lowering your body position and isolating the muscles of the inner thigh. Many people think that the only reason for lowering the body position is to increase aerodynamics—and to some extent, that is true—but you will notice that by lowering your body properly, the upper portion of your body becomes almost superfluous to the skating process. It becomes quiet. The muscles of the upper leg and hip region begin doing the majority of the work, thus drawing much, if not all, the body's energy. The lower position also allows the quadriceps and gluteus to push more effectively, as it is more suited to their natural range of motion.

What I mean by "lowering the body" is this: Bend forward at the waist (imagine a speed skater) and lower your center of gravity slightly. Your back should be flat (imagine yourself sitting on a racing bicycle) but angled upward. It's important that you keep the back straight. Poor back position leads to lower back strain. What you end up with is a position in which your chest is directly above your knees with each push and glide, while the head is forced to tilt upward so that you can look ahead.

From this position, the push phase is one of the only functions the body can perform optimally, form following function. The legs cannot go forward with any sort of power, only backward. The low-slung body is counterbalanced by swinging your arms in an easy back-and-forth, half-windmill fashion. This action provides momentum as well as that balance dynamic. When you push from the lowered position, notice how much more strength you get from each push.

You will first notice the benefits of this powerful new push during the glide phase. Your speed obviously will be higher. Your glide will be longer and even more controlled (a skate is easier to control with a modicum of speed). There really isn't a modification you will have to make to your glide, other than to resist the urge to begin another push stroke before the momentum slows down.

One drawback of the power stroke is that it can't be done all the time, except by incredibly fit individuals. You will feel a definite burn in your upper thighs, the result of spending time in what is essentially a crouched position. It's not a harmful burn, merely the buildup of lactic acid that is your muscles telling you that they are getting tired. You will find that in the course of an in-line session, this burn will come and go regularly, depending upon whether you are resting (skating casually in an upright position) or using a power stroke.

As you become more fit, and your muscles become stronger and better acquainted with the rigors of in-line skating, you will find that you can stay in the power-stroke position for longer and longer periods of time. Until then, the best way to work on that power stroke is to skate alternately in the upright and power-stroke position. What I like to do is skate upright when I find myself in traffic—cars, people, dogs, bike trails—and use the power stroke when the pavement is free and clear and inviting me to air it out.

Power-Stroke Drills

Before we move on, here are a few drills to refine your power stroke.

Push Drill. Skaters very often make the mistake of pushing off with the ball of their foot. This isn't surprising, as most natural forms of push-off (running, walking) involve using the forefoot. However, one primary function of the in-line boot is to negate this tendency so that power can be distributed through the entire foot. Attempts to use the forefoot lead to strained Achilles tendons and reduced power in the push. Additionally, using the forefoot reduces the amount of pushing surface. The push, you remember, is done with the all wheels on the ground, not just two or three.

To combat this tendency, overexaggerate the heel's emphasis in the push phase. Disregarding that it feels unnatural, perform a series of lateral pushes that overemphasize the act of placing the heel on the ground and driving off of that point. It should feel as if your heel is trying to push the wheels directly beneath it into the ground.

Weight lifters perform a similar motion when they perform squats, the exercise that is often compared to a deep knee bend, but with a barbell on your shoulders. As in skating, they find that they lose power if they try to use the toes as the driving force. Using the toes strains the back and puts unnecessary pressure on the Achilles' tendon. By driving with the heels, however, the center of gravity stays directly over the driving point and the weight is lifted more simply. In simple terms, that means you'll get more power from your push if you use your heel.

Glide Drill. Your glide can be much more efficient and longer by giving it more direction. Instead of merely placing your skates on the ground to begin the glide, drive forward out of the push with your knee leading the way. Pretend that you're in a marching band and that the knee must come up to bend at a precise 90-degree angle before you lower it to place your wheels on the ground.

Why? The act of lifting your knee forces your weight back. You glide more efficiently in that fashion. Many people land on their toes, with their weight too far forward, which has the effect of braking their forward momentum in a very subtle fashion. And while the effect may feel minimal, the point of the drill is to maximize that glide, which in turn makes your power stroke all the more powerful.

Just remember that this is a drill. The overexaggeration of lifting your knee is not something you would do normally.

Slalom Technique

The closest thing to in-line skating slalom technique is snow skiing. Every movement, with the inclusion of edging, weight shifting, and the fundamentals of turning, is similar. There will be a longer discussion of those comparisons later (in chapter 11). At that time the focus will be on using in-line skating to prepare you for the ski season. Now, however, it's truly helpful if you can somehow find a way to put thoughts of slaloming on snow skis out of your mind. Why? The reasons we will discuss slaloming have more to do with self-defense on crowded or obstacle-strewn streets and any potential future in in-line hockey you may harbor. So if at all possible, think of this discussion in those terms.

Let's start with the fairly obvious: The slalom position is an upright one. Slaloming from the power-stroke position is all but impossible (though not entirely, it just takes a great deal of concentration and has a higher potential for peril). So stand up straight and loose (knees bent, arms relaxed, eyes forward, skates parallel) as you chart the obstacles through which you plan to slalom. It's worth noting that you'll probably already be in this position, so it shouldn't take much effort.

Get ready to turn. Now, before you begin, it's worth knowing that there are two ways to perfect the slalom. Many people learn only one or the other, but I think it's more helpful if you actually learn both. Again, the idea is to train your body to smoothly dodge potential pratfalls. Knowing more than one way to achieve that can only be to your benefit.

Skate-to-Skate

This is the simpler of the two techniques to explain, but whether or not it feels more difficult to actually perform is up to you. Those individuals comfortable skating on one leg will likely enjoy this technique more.

Begin by setting up a small slalom course on your practice area. For now, try to practice your slalom on a level course. The basics are easier to pick up on if done without the influx of speed brought on by downhills.

So you've set up your course—maybe it's a few orange traffic cones or just a few random marks on the pavement, as long as it's not around immobile objects—and you skate into your first turn. Using the skate-to-skate method of weight transfer, lift the unweighted skate (the one *not* carving the turn) and lift it off the ground entirely—not a lot, maybe just an inch or two, but enough so that the entire act of skating around that cone is being accomplished by just one skate. Before you come out of the turn, put the airborne foot back on the ground and give a quick push to propel you into the next turn. Between turns, skate on both skates.

What benefit does skate-to-skate allow? The turning arc will be tighter, because only one skate is being forced to carve the turn. Also, the force generated by pushing as you come out of the turn will give you more power than will skating with two skates on the ground. This is the technique to use when generating locomotion is important, like when skating on a flat surface. I also think it's important to practice this technique because you never know when you will be forced to make a sudden, one-footed turn. By practicing it ahead of time, such a movement will not throw off your balance. And if you want to get right down to it, the skate-to-skate looks really cool because you go fast and you make tight turns.

Smooth Carving

This is a slower but more graceful method of carving a turn. Basically, smooth carving is a series of continuous, flowing half moons that take you around obstacles with effortlessness. It is the turn for those who treasure aesthetics. People who perform this technique look as if they were born with skates grafted to their ankles. Because it doesn't generate its own speed, it is a technique better suited to downhill skating than flatland skating. However, practice first on a flat surface.

The movement is simple, but making it look great takes time and patience. Start by attacking the same slalom course you practiced the skate-to-skate on. As you head into the turn, slip one skate in front of the other and weight it to carve the turn. This is the same movement you make when carving a lazy 180-degree turn. Make sure to keep the unweighted skate on the ground. It will provide stability as you come out of the turn and shift your weight to the other skate.

Remember, with two skates on the ground, carving a tight turn is much more difficult. That is why smooth carving is not about tight turns. It's about continuous turns that expend as little energy as possible. The turn should never look sharp or quirky, merely seamless. This takes a bit of practice, but those who can perfect this technique will see dividends in their overall style.

Skating on One Leg

Using the skate-to-skate slalom technique, we touched on the concept of skating on one leg. And while this may seem a conceit—something akin to riding a bicycle with no hands—skating on one skate actually fulfills a very functional purpose, namely, teaching the muscles of the shin, ankle, and foot to balance perfectly atop the center of your wheels. Weight distribution of this sort is key in in-line skating.

Skating on one leg is more of a drill than anything else. That's obvious, seeing as how the push and glide is dependent upon two skates. But so important is the concept of proper weight distribution that it's worth trying something radical to perfect it.

So begin by taking one skate off. Keep a shoe on that foot, of course, something comfortable that you can work out in. You should be standing on your practice area, then, with one foot in a skate and the other on the ground. From there it's a matter of pushing off with the unskated foot and gliding as you roll along. Try to make each glide go as straight as possible and to last until you run entirely out of momentum. Like most drills, this sort of exaggeration will help you realize where you need to make corrections in your form. Alternate legs, making sure to spend equal time perfecting the balance of each.

Speed Can Be Your Friend

It's not necessary to harbor an affinity for speed skating to enjoy the thrill of speed. Take note that *speed* and *downhill* are not necessarily synonymous. All good skaters have a fundamental comfort level about executing difficult maneuvers at high speed. This can mean slaloming or skating backward, to a lesser extent. It can also mean wide, arcing turns and even the occasional jump to avoid a sudden object in your path (jumping, it should be pointed out, is always a last resort). The proper attitude to take toward speed is that it's best enjoyed when it's not reckless. Too many people feel that the best way to pretend they can skate competently is to zip off at a super-high speed, not taking into account that they have the ability neither to stop without crashing nor to prevent themselves from crashing into others and causing injury.

A few rules about speed:

1. *Don't force it.* While it's important to feel comfortable with speed, let your tolerance build along with your talent. Remember your first day on skates? Remember how even the slight forward movement you experienced felt overwhelming? Well, just because you feel comfortable on skates now is no license to speed. If you want to go fast, slowly allow yourself to be comfortable tolerating higher and higher speeds.

2. *Never let yourself feel out of control.* In control and out of control are subjective sensations. Professional speed skaters can zip along at 35 mph and feel right at home, sure that they can dodge any mishap. Good speed skaters even brag that they are so relaxed at speeds that they can roll right through a crash and escape without a scratch. Then there are new skaters, those who feel hopelessly out of control at just 10 mph. These folks are best served by knowing their limits. Chances are, if you feel out of control, a crash is imminent.

3. *Prepare for speed.* This means proper equipment maintenance so that your equipment doesn't fail at high speeds. There's no quicker way to wash away confidence in your ability to handle speed than to suddenly start doubting your equipment. It means lacing and buckling your boots properly, so that instability is never an issue. It means knowing the terrain—if you're skating on a new patch of pavement, and you wish to go fast, make sure that gravel and pavement cracks don't become an issue.

4. *Learn to enjoy speed.* If you come to enjoy the visceral sensation of effortless speed and the wind whistling past your helmet straps, you will begin to relax. As always, this will make you a better skater and enhance your overall skating experience.

The steps you have taken in this chapter to advance from beginner to intermediate have undoubtedly stretched you as a skater. Be proud of trying, even if these new techniques are not coming with-

out difficulty. From here, the next step is into a variety of other levels, whether that means using in-line skating as a form of fitness,
playing hockey, speed skating, in-line dancing, or even extreme skating. While those brands of skating might have been impossible to
conceptualize achieving not long ago, you will find that you have the
technique and skills now to take the next step with ease.

7

SKATING FOR FITNESS

Or, Having Fun Getting Fit

Skating, in all its guises, is most commonly used by adults as a form of fitness. The reasons for this are many, but they have a great deal more to do with skating's mix of fun and athleticism than anything else. In many ways, I think the fact that so many see it as a form of fitness pays the sport a great compliment. Not that fitness is necessarily drudgery, but many people see it that way and avoid exercise because of this. Why work out, they ask, when watching TV enriches my life so much more? Thus, in-line skating is a form of fitness that doesn't know it's a form of fitness, and its proponents don't really know it's a form of fitness, either.

What is it, then? It's play. George Sheehan, the late running philosopher, said of his sport: "There are as many reasons for running as there are days in a year. But mostly I run because I am an animal and a child, an artist and saint. Everyone is an athlete. The only difference is that some are in training and some are not. Running makes you an athlete in all areas of life—trained in the basics, prepared for whatever comes, ready to fill each hour and deal with that decisive moment" (*Runner's World* calendar, 1994).

The same, I think, is true of in-line skating. We are all part animal, part child, part artist, part saint. Rolling along at speed is innately wondrous, a form of expression not found in methods of fitness like tennis or racquetball. We are all athletes as well. The body at rest is more relaxed and, some would say, more happy. But the body in motion is a more natural state, and that sensation of being and doing that derives from movement is a natural high.

Getting back to those goals we discussed in the early chapters, was one of yours to add an in-line regimen to your fitness lifestyle? If

Twenty minutes of in-line skating lets you burn about 200 calories.

so, did you want to tone muscles, lose weight, or just plain get that heart rate up for hours on end? Well, the beauty of in-line skating is that you can do all of those, without doing much more than skating normally.

Of course, there's the added tenet of discipline when it comes to weight loss. Exercise alone will not permanently trim pounds and fat. If you want to keep it off, you must learn to eat well at the same time. Eating well is the same as eating right. That generally means a diet high in carbohydrates (60 percent of daily intake), with the remainder an equal amount of protein and fat (20 percent each), to make up a balanced daily diet. Water is incredibly important, as a well-hydrated body not only operates better, but looks better also. There are some folks who say eight glasses of water a day is necessary, but I find that a hard rule to stick with. Try the technique of a good friend of mine if the thought of sucking down eight glasses of water each day seems a bit burdensome. Instead of quantifying water intake that way, he simply makes it a point to stop at a water fountain each time he passes one while at work. He doesn't gulp like a camel, either. Instead, he takes a few chaste sips and goes on his way. Simple, and over the course of the day, it adds up.

Losing Weight

Probably the biggest thing on people's minds when they start skating for fitness is that elusive question: "How much weight am I going to lose?" Many people seem to think they could afford to drop a few pounds. If you're one of those people, in-line skating will do wonders for helping you drop weight. To do that, however, you may have to reevaluate your definition of weight loss. More exactly, you may need to reevaluate the process of weight loss. There is a commonly held misconception about fitness and losing weight that goes something like this: "If I eat less, then I will ingest fewer calories, and then I will lose weight—particularly those love handles and cottage cheese thighs."

Wrong. "By eating less you actually slow your metabolism down, so the body is burning fewer calories," says Dr. Herman Falsetti, an Irvine, California, cardiologist who has worked with several top triathletes, cyclists, and runners, "and dieting does nothing in the way of increasing muscle tone and definition. The only way to achieve optimal fitness, and by that I mean weight loss and increased muscle mass, tone and definition, is to incorporate some form of regular cardiovascular exercise into your workout routine."

Which is where in-line skating comes in. A 1994 study by the University of Massachusetts Exercise Science Department found that in-line skating burned as many calories as easy running. The study of twenty men and women found that their caloric consumption was, on the average, between 450 and 600 calories per hour on in-lines. This computes to anywhere from seven to ten calories per minute. In addition, in-line skating is a proven form of cardiovascular exercise, working the heart and lungs. Studies have shown that adults should exercise cardiovascularly a minimum of twenty minutes per session, three sessions per week, in order to achieve cardiovascular health. Of course, factors such as diet content enter into the mix, but the point is that you can burn somewhere in the neighborhood of 200 calories and achieve the satisfaction of knowing that your heart and lungs are being honed, simply by rolling around your block for twenty minutes, three times a week.

So why stop there? In-line skating is not drudgery. Even the most churlish individuals have a hard time fighting a smile when they strap on a pair of skates. As I have said before, there's something engaging and free-spirited about the sport of in-lining that brings out the kid in all of us. We don't feel like we're exercising on in-lines, we feel like we are playing. It's a sport that feels almost too fun to be real exercise, and I think that's important. If what you do for exercise is something that you feel is fun instead of a short-term prison sentence, you will be more likely to do it more often—and longer. You may take your skates out on a day that you had not even planned on working out. Something inside you just felt the urge to skate, and you followed it. If you happen to achieve muscle tone, heart and lung condition, and a certain amount of caloric consumption in the process, then all the better.

Fitting In-Line Skating into Your Regimen

You will notice the word *regimen* in the title of this section. Well, it really should not be there. Regimens are self-inflicted disciplines that imply little in the way of fun. In-lining won't feel like any sort of regimen. It will feel like fun. You may even discount in-lining when it comes to fitness for that reason. So let's put aside terms like *regimen* and *workout* and *training* (very Rocky Balboa-ish), because the connotations are grim to many. Instead, let's call what you are about to do on in-lines simply *skating*. Runners call their sport running. Cyclists say they are going riding. Skaters should skate. This blurs the distinction between the pain and suffering most often associated with fitness, replacing it with the glimmer of fun that is skating.

For those of you who enjoy a solid fitness program, the question may be: "How does skating fit into my life right now?" More specifically, how does it fit into your current fitness regime (there's that word again)? If you have a fitness club membership or own a mountain bike or enjoy a swim now and again at the local pool, where does in-lining fit into the mix? The first thing you have to do when answering that question is avoid an all-or-nothing answer. Don't figure that just because you now skate for fitness, you have to suddenly disavow participation in other activities. I would counsel continuing what you normally do, whether it be aerobics or running or swimming, but substitute skating a few days a week. For instance, if you do aerobics four times a week, make skating a regular part of your life by doing aerobics three times a week and skating that one other time. The change will energize you and add a facet of playfulness. If you choose to add more in-line skating, then work it in slowly. Avoid adding in-line skating on top of your regular program. For instance, don't do aerobics four times a week and feel like you have to skate four times a week as well.

For those without any form of fitness program beyond channel surfing, don't enter into an in-line fitness program pell-mell. The mistake many people make is to begin a fitness program with the most wondrous of intentions, then burn out within a mere two or three weeks. Health clubs report that new memberships skyrocket after the first of the year, when New Year's resolutions are strong and everyone is rushing in to burn off unwanted pounds. But what happens? The gyms are empty again by the first of February.

So if you are starting a new program with skating as its centerpiece, hoping all the while to lose weight and increase muscle tone, give yourself modest goals at first. Tell yourself that skating just once a week is fine. Increase it to twice or three times a week after a month or so. Instead of jumping up to four or five times from there, try increasing either the amount of time or the intensity of your three sessions. If, after in-lining becomes an ingrained part of your life, you feel the urge to begin doing it five or six days a week, try to keep it casual. Don't beat yourself up if you miss a day. That sort of compulsivity robs you of the joy you can derive from in-lining.

The ideal state is one where in-lining—or some other form of fitness; experts say that diversity in training is what keeps people interested—is so ingrained into your day that it doesn't feel unnatural to slip your skates on and go for a spin. If studies have shown that successful individuals invariably include an hour of fitness in their day, then that should tell you that you may want to do the same. If that means getting up an hour earlier or exercising before lunch or in the evening, well, why not? The addition of a workout will add to your quality of life.

Picture this scenario: You're in your office or at a meeting, having one of those mornings that never seems to end. You're obviously not burning up a whole lot of calories beyond mere nervous tension by sitting there on your behind. And you know that if you go out and eat a large lunch, you'll be falling asleep at your desk by midafternoon. So, you tell yourself, looking out the window and seeing the sun shining, why don't I go for a quick skate? If you keep your pads and skates in the trunk of your car, it's just a few minutes' walk, a quick change, then you're on your way. You can munch some carrot sticks and a piece of fruit when you return—don't skip lunch altogether. Your body needs that midday fuel.

Imagine how lighthearted you'll feel when you get back. Blood pumping, mind freed from distractions, life looking just that much easier. Maybe your job won't feel as oppressive after a good skate, which translates into better performance, which translates into a better performance review, which could translate into a raise as well.

Still not convinced to adopt some sort of in-line (or other form of) fitness routine into your daily life? Then how about this scenario: You let yourself get a little too heavy. You eat poorly. You drink too much coffee and alcohol, thereby raising your blood pressure (as if everything else hasn't done it already). So you have a heart attack. The result: time off from work for convalescence, a forced change in your lifestyle, medical bills, and the burden of pain and suffering on your family.

This isn't to make exercise the be-all and end-all of your existence, and it's not to point out that a few hours spent exercising each day isn't just a good thing to do. Instead, it's to point out that not exercising is an almost irresponsible act. Exercise isn't pulling teeth. It's a way of improving your quality of life and reducing the chance that something physically bad might happen to you.

A Note on Diet

The common idea of dieting is slowly starving yourself to lose weight. However, starvation dieting is actually detrimental to the process. It turns out that when the body experiences a lack of food, the metabolism slows down, which makes it harder to burn calories.

A curious by-product of starvation dieting is bad breath. It comes about because the brain, which uses only sugar—not fat—as a fuel source, commands the muscles to turn themselves into sugar if no other food enters the body (early signs that this is happening include light-headedness and headaches). A result of that muscle breakdown is an abundance of protein in the system, which overwhelms the kidneys. Instead of being secreted by urine, it comes out in the form of body odor and bad breath.

The proper way to diet is to combine exercise and eating habits. Men should never lose more than 2 pounds a week; women, no more than 1 to 1½. The best thing to do is to eat a big breakfast, smaller lunch, and light dinner. This holds especially true for business travelers, when there is a tendency to eat later at night. If you go to bed with 1,800 calories in your stomach, there's no way your body can burn it off. It will turn to fat overnight.

However, life and business being what they are, eating a big meal late at night is sometimes inevitable. The thing to do in that instance is try to minimize alcohol and coffee intake (they both cause dehydration and interrupt sleep patterns), then start the next day with a light workout.

A mistake people often make when dieting is that when they slip up and eat too much—putting their resolution to diet aside—they tend to go to the other extreme to make up for it. They binge one day and starve the next. Avoid this habit. When you're overly hungry you're more likely to stuff yourself at mealtime than if you're not. If you happen to step away from your diet for a day or a week, quietly resume it when you're ready. Do it at your own pace. Be your own disciplinarian.

Setting Goals

Take a look at those goals again. Read them, even refine them. There is an aimlessness to any skating program that lacks a center, so when looking at those goals, be cognizant of what your focus is. Whether you skate for fun or fitness or the thrill of pulling backside air off a ramp, it helps to know why you are skating. Again, this isn't to make the sport ponderous, but—and this is especially true as it applies to skating for fitness—having a goal gives you both something to strive for and a marker to chart progress. Within the realm of fitness skating, ask yourself where you're going and what you skate for. Are you skating to lose weight? If so, how much would you like to lose, and by when? Are you skating to increase lean muscle mass? Then have your body fat level checked and decide how much fat you plan to replace with muscles and by what date. Make your goals reasonable. Don't try to lose 30 pounds in thirty days, because you will fail; you will become disgusted with skating and disgusted with yourself, and you will return to the couch and the remote control until the next time the urge to exercise arises.

Keep it simple. This is a long-term proposition: 30 pounds lost is 30 pounds lost, whether it happens in one month or twelve. A sample goal might go something like this: "Within six months I would like to lose 10 pounds and get in the habit of skating three times a week." Or: "I would like to become a competitive speed skater. To do that I must increase my endurance base, lose 15 pounds of body fat, and build skating strength by increasing muscle mass in my thighs and glutes."

Start by breaking your goals down into daily or weekly subgoals that will lead to accomplishment of the main goal. For instance, if your goal is to lose 10 pounds, ponder what it will take to achieve that. At a subgoal level, that might translate to cutting daily caloric consumption or reducing the amount of fat in each meal (we will talk more about diet later, but remember that the recommended amount of fat in your daily caloric intake should not exceed 20 percent).

You will find that if you break very big goals into small, reasonable, attainable steps, getting to the promised land will be that much easier. As the old saying goes, a journey of a thousand miles begins with a single step.

You get the point. Whether the aim of your program is basic, weight-loss fitness or something of a more serious ilk, take a few minutes and set goals. Really think about them before committing, making sure that you allow yourself a reasonable level of time to reach the goal.

Including Rewards

Too often, fitness is a pursuit without rewards. An Olympic athlete knows that if he or she trains an entire lifetime and is imbued with a certain amount of natural talent, then there's a pretty good chance the Olympic Games could be viewed as a goal. Likewise, a football player dreams of the Super Bowl, and baseball players grow up dreaming of hitting the winning home run in the seventh game of the World Series.

But what about the guy or gal who works a whole year to lose that elusive 30 pounds? Sure, folks will remark that he or she looks good, or the person's clothes will fit better, but those are really external things. I think when you reach the end of a long-sought goal, you have to give yourself a reward. Why? Because it's a mental carrot that will keep you motivated while you're laboring to see that goal become a reality.

Say that your goal is to increase your *VO₂ max* (the maximum amount of oxygen your lungs can inhale effectively). And since you know that VO₂ max is a by-product of weight as well as cardiovascular fitness, you swear to lose 5 pounds in the long run and go for an hourlong skate each week. Let's say that it takes you three months to reach that goal. It's my belief that after reaching your goal, you treat yourself. Maybe it's an extra hour of sleep on Saturday morning or a new CD or a special article of clothing that will now fit you better. Whatever the reward might be, make sure you think of a way to reward yourself for a job well done. Sometimes the sacrifice that comes with a goal is only tolerable if you know that there is a pot of gold at the end of that rainbow.

What happens a lot of times when I try to set goals without offering myself a reward at the end is that I lose interest. If I know that I need to lift weights to increase my lean muscle mass, while at the same time decrease the amount of fat in my diet, I'll most likely stick with the program awhile, and at first it will be easy, but sooner or later there will be the temptation to skip a workout or two or three and to go overboard on pizza and beer. What I need in times like that (besides a call to discipline and moderation) is a reminder—in the form of a reward—of why I'm chasing the goal in the first place. If I can tell myself that there's something special in store, well, I'll be more diligent.

The Best Way to Burn Fat

We all want to be lean, but what's the best way to get that way? Or maybe, what's the very best way in the world for a skater to burn fat? Skate slowly. By skating at a comfortable pace (a good gauge is if you can skate consistently and carry on a conversation), the body burns fat as an energy source instead of sugar (in the form of glycogen). Because the body gets plenty of oxygen at that level, endurance is increased as the oxygen-rich blood is pumped into muscles. While body fat is being decreased, lean muscle mass is being increased. Talk about your win-win situations.

Skating at an easy pace burns fat and increases endurance.

It's worth noting that burning fat and losing weight are often two different things. Remember, when you burn body fat, lean muscle mass is increased. But muscle weighs more than fat, so you might not see the expected results on your bathroom scale. After three weeks of a program you might look down at that needle and wonder why you haven't lost—or why you even may have gained—weight. Here are two things to remember. First, if your clothes fit you better, then you're losing body fat. "They'll start to hang on you more," is what Dr. Falsetti tells his patients. Which is nice, because tight clothing doesn't carry the same level of comfort as loose, well-fitted clothes. The second thing to remember is that if you want to lose weight, combine your increased exercise with a reduction in calories.

The Best Way to Get Fast

We will discuss increasing speed for racing in later chapters, but the fastest way to get ready for racing is to train your body to adapt to the stressors it will encounter during a race. How? Skate fast. Skate fast because the body must learn to function capably in a state of oxygen debt.

During a race, the body is in a constant state of oxygen debt, burning sugar as a fuel source instead of fat. Muscles are being torn down as the lack of oxygen leads to a buildup of lactic acid. Stressful as it sounds, that is the level at which elite endurance athletes compete and which they must learn to tolerate. It's not necessary, however, to be an elite athlete to see a vast improvement in your ability to skate quickly. There are several methods of training that will make you a faster skater and increase your body's ability to tolerate life outside the comfort zone.

It is important to mix long, easy fat-burning/endurance-building workouts with short, hard oxygen debt (known more commonly as *anaerobic*) workouts in order to become a competitive skater. This is also true if you wish to skate as a form of weight reduction. For example, if you go out for a hard twenty minutes at an anaerobic pace, your body burns nothing but sugar. As soon as you finish the workout and eat a meal, whatever weight reduction benefits you derived from the workout are gone, because the meal replaced all those sugars you burned. However, with long, slow sessions, you burn fat, which is not so easily replaced.

Training Smarter, Not Harder

Want to train more efficiently, knowing that each moment of each workout counts toward the greater goal in a definitive way? Invest in a heart rate monitor. You will be able to more accurately gauge perceived exertion levels to decide whether the day's workout is being performed in an appropriate manner. Let me explain. Traditional training techniques specify that athletes develop fitness by training "hard-easy"—that is, working to a perceived maximum level one day, then bringing the intensity level way down so that muscles can rest before being subjected to another hard workout (muscle growth takes place during the rest cycle, which builds it up, rather than the exercise cycle, which tears it down).

However, "certain muscle functions," says Dr. Falsetti, "are a byproduct of heart rate rather than perceived exertion." Falsetti goes on to say that it is possible to set the exact number of beats per minute you should attain to achieve maximum efficiency during interval sessions (90 to 100 percent of maximum heart rate), recovery session (less than 60 percent of max), and fat-burning/endurance-building sessions (60 to 70 percent). These figures are a function of maximum heart rate, which is most accurately gauged through something known as a twelve-lead stress test. The twelve-lead stress test is a complex procedure involving a treadmill and your doctor. An easier way to discover your maximum heart rate is to subtract your age from the number 220. It won't be as accurate, but it is close enough to roughly approximate exertion with a heart rate monitor. Dr. Falsetti cautions, however, that the twelve-lead test is preferable whenever possible.

"Without knowing your maximum heart rate," Dr. Falsetti adds, stressing the importance of a thoroughly accurate test, "the concept of hard-easy is flawed, because it's so subjective. Your hard days feel hard and your easy days feel easy. But many times I have found that athletes were working at 85 percent when they should have been working at 95 percent. And on days when they should have been recovering, there were times when their heart rate was well above 80 percent, which negated any recovery they were trying to incur."

Just what is a heart rate monitor? It is a thin band worn around your chest during exercise that transmits your heart rate to an electronic monitor worn on your wrist. It can be tiresome to constantly look at your wrist and monitor your heart rate, but if you have a limited amount of time and are interested in maximizing fitness by not wasting a workout, then they are a worthwhile investment.

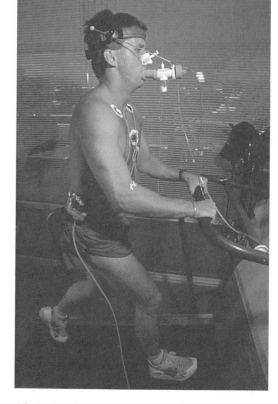

The twelve-lead stress test commonly used by exercise physiologists is the most exact method of determining heart and lung function.

When an individual starts training within the fat-burning zone of 60 to 70 percent of his or her maximum heart rate, say three times a week for forty minutes each time, results will happen within a matter of weeks, Dr. Falsetti says.

There are drawbacks to heart monitors. For instance, when dehydration sets in, the heart rate goes up. I remember once when I was out for a run on a hot day, and even though I was barely jogging, my heart rate monitor had me pegged at an almost anaerobic threshold figure (the point at which increased heart rate causes oxygen debt). So be aware of that factor.

Another factor to watch out for is simple fatigue. When the body is tired, heart rate increases. What this means is that a heart rate monitor is most effective for short, vigorous workouts or midlength slow workouts. Start putting in the hour-long and two-hour-long skates and you'll find the heart rate monitor largely irrelevant.

Putting it All Together

When you design a program, make sure to do it around your goals. As an example: The purpose of this chapter is to build fit skaters instead of speed skaters, so many of you will want to ignore the parts about oxygen debt. Whatever your aim, remember to start small. Don't try to do too much, too soon.

It's important to note that fitness is not a one-time thing, to be achieved, then forgotten. Fitness is something to be maintained (hence the use of the term *lifestyle*) for a prolonged period, and hopefully a lifetime. Don't bite off more than you can chew by setting a needlessly ambitious goal for your fitness program. Think of something modest, but just out of your reach, then work toward it. When you attain it, set another goal. Always keep in mind the importance of striving anew each day. Also, remember that there's no need to set your standards too high. Who's going to notice if you achieve that goal? Probably not too many people except you. Likewise, should you fail, not too many people will know. The difference is that if you strive too high and fail, something inside you may lose interest in trying anymore. This sport is too hard, you'll tell yourself. But when you set manageable goals, achieve them, then move on to more goals, you'll be in a rejuvenated frame of mind. The world will be your oyster, and you'll be ready to take on greatness.

Maybe you just like to roll around on your skates. Maybe discussions of aerobic and anaerobic and heart rate monitors are a bit eso-

teric, too much the realm of the overly intense individual. Maybe all you want to do is find time in your busy week to skate for half an hour on three or four different occasions, without worrying about the need for planning your training. Maybe thinking of skating as a viable form of fitness comparable to running and cycling still doesn't mesh with what you perceive as fitness. For you, skating is fun—a kid's game. Period. Don't be ashamed to admit it. Most recreational skaters feel that way. Though in-lining is well on its way to achieving worldwide acceptance as a method of recreation, it's still not popular as a way of getting in shape.

So be a trendsetter. Put together your program, using the information on goal setting, fat burning, anaerobic factors, and the function of heart rate. Give it a month—at least—to see what transpires. Don't fret if you don't lose weight initially; that's just a case of muscle weight replacing fat. A more telling indicator that you are on the right track will be your clothes. How do they fit? Are they feeling a bit baggy after a month of in-line fitness?

Probably. So stick with your program for another month. When the weight starts to come off—and it will—watch in amazement at how your friends react when you inform them that you lost those pounds through in-line skating. You can tell them how fun it is. And how you can skate backward. And how it does not even feel like a workout because it feels like such a mental release just to slip into a pair of skates and glide effortlessly along the pavement, your cares drifting away like the wind pushing back your hair.

Tell them these things and maybe, just maybe, you will have a few new skating partners.

8

CHECK!

In-Line Hockey 101

Without a doubt, one of the biggest stimulus to in-line's phenomenal growth has been the surge in in-line hockey participation. A fortuitous surge in popularity in ice hockey among the American public has translated into a groundswell of fascination with pucks and skates and sticks that has benefited in-line hockey in a very big way. Where once roller hockey was seen as a weak sister of ice hockey, played on roller skates by a tiny group of faithful believers, the sport is now—especially with the introduction of in-lines—booming. Two men's professional leagues are in existence (Roller Hockey International and the Continental In-Line Hockey League), with many of the players coming from the National Hockey League, using the in-line season as a means of both fitness and competitive honing.

Why is in-line hockey such a great game? It just is. Like basketball, the action is nonstop, and the finesse element makes it possible for players to develop skills that transcend brute force and speed elements. Like baseball, in-line hockey is a game that kids love for its fun and adults love for its intricacy. Mostly, though, with ice hockey on the rise (the 1990s version of what NBA basketball was in the 1980s), more and more people have an appreciation for the game. They know the teams and the players. They know the plays and the penalties. And when the fans start identifying with stuff like that, they start to dream of doing it themselves. More than any other facet of in-line skating, in-line hockey has a vital connection to a professional sport. Somehow that makes the allure of participating in the game all the more intense, because you get to imagine that you're one of the greats—Gretzky or Lemieux—when you thwart a sure

Getting the puck in the net is what hockey's all about.

goal or fire a pass. And if you chance to score . . . well, the imagination runs wild.

There are, of course, differences between in-line hockey and ice hockey. Ice hockey players will tell you that the 1/8-inch blade on an ice hockey skate gives you a better edge, thus allowing you to turn more sharply and crisply. Given that, plus the playing surface, ice hockey players also move faster. Also, in-line hockey uses both a ball and special roller puck, neither of which has quite the zing of an ice hockey puck when it comes off the player's stick.

But in-line hockey is by no means an inferior sport. When played indoors, the game is played on the same size rink and in many cases features the same "boards" and penalty boxes as ice hockey. Players wear the same pads, use the same hockey sticks, and shoot into the same size goal as they do in ice hockey. In-line hockey is fast and furious, demanding that skaters possess superb skating ability to better deal with the myriad turns and stops that comprise hockey's stop-and-go action. In-line hockey builds the same muscles as ice hockey, which also means that top aerobic and anaerobic conditioning is required of all athletes. There are a million comparisons and contrasts to the two, and the bottom line is this: In-line hockey is a legitimate sport, one that's exciting and demanding. As a workout, it will kick your butt.

In fact, ice hockey requires a greater deal of finesse and less actual muscle use from skaters as they perform maneuvers. Roller hockey, because the skater has less control with wheels than with blades, requires greater muscle use. In some ways, the level of technical skill is higher also. Consider that ice hockey requires players to master only two stopping techniques, the snowplow and the hockey stop. In-line hockey requires that players use both front and back snowplows, the T-stop, and the hockey stop. These stops actually bring into use all the major muscles of the lower leg and torso.

The purpose of this chapter isn't to define the rules of the game. Hockey is hockey, and this isn't the place to digress on the intricacies of the sport. What's more important, however, is how the sport applies to you, the player.

Not for Men Only

Throughout this chapter I will be using the male pronoun to describe hockey players. I want to make it clear not only that I think women are capable of playing as well as men, but that many do. Hockey is

Proper Way to Grasp a Hockey Stick

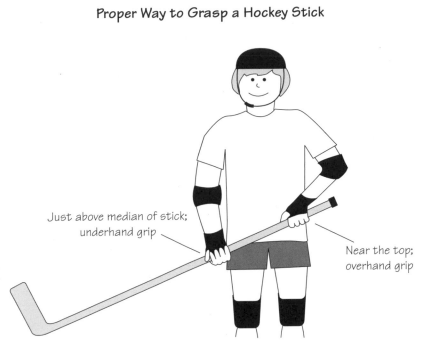

Just above median of stick; underhand grip

Near the top; overhand grip

Proper Hockey Stick Height
(Floor to chin with skates on)

one of those great sports that emphasizes speed and finesse. Women may lack some of the brawn that men tend to rely on, but that could actually work to their advantage. For instance, instead of getting checked into the boards by some big bruiser, the smarter female players have developed the solid skating skills necessary to gingerly evade such goons. Instead of getting trapped against the boards, letting a loose puck get stolen away, the better female players have developed the stick-handling skills to hang onto it. Finally, those women who find themselves totally turned off by the thought of any of the physical contact should consider that the position of goalie is a noncontact, highly skilled position in which wits and reflexes count for as much as brawn.

So go to it, ladies. Just because hockey has a reputation as a physical sport in which bruises and bumps are taken as a matter of course, that doesn't mean you can't play, too.

Equipment

There are basic pieces of equipment every player should have. Other than skates, the most important ones you can own are a stick of

Either a ball or a regulation puck can be used for in-line hockey

Face-Off Circle

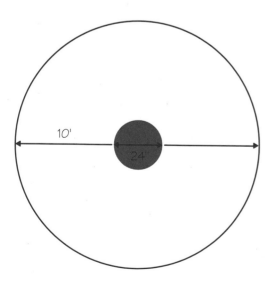

proper length and a helmet that protects the back and sides of your head. Even if you have an in-line helmet, be aware that hockey helmets, like hockey skates, have a few refinements added to their design to facilitate better hockey. In the case of hockey helmets, they are a bit different than normal in-line helmets because they cover a bit more of the head and offer a little less padding on top. The result is a helmet that fits your head snugly, unobtrusively, and in a lightweight manner that will facilitate playing a long, tough game.

Something you probably won't have is a hockey stick. When selecting a stick, it's best to take your skates to the store with you, because stick length depends on the skater's height. Ideally, the end of the stick should come between your chin and the middle of your chest as you stand with your skates on. It's worth pointing out that whether you're right-handed or left-handed should not affect whether you use a right-handed or left-handed stick. Try several, and see what feels best to you.

Other pads and pieces of equipment you might consider: Shin and ankle pads, gloves, mouth guards, wrist protectors, and both a puck and a ball (depending upon the type of playing surface, either can be used: balls are used in street hockey, pucks on smoother indoor surfaces).

A Few Basic Skills

When you play, and when you prepare to play, it's important to have a solid grasp of certain fundamentals that will make your game better. The idea is to incorporate these fundamentals into your playing until they become second nature. You want your body to know how to use these skills without having to think about it.

The ready position. This is just the basic "let's play" stance you'll assume before a face-off or even when you're trying to anticipate your opponent's next move. Stand with your head up, eyes taking in all of the rink. Keep those ankles and knees flexed lightly, with your feet shoulder-width apart. The idea here is to incorporate the concept of balance into your play. When you're balanced, you're prepared for any move. When you're balanced, you can move in any direction—forward, backward, left, right—without giving it too much thought. When you're balanced, you can do anything.

Explosion. The ability to make a fast, explosive movement off the puck is what separates dynamic players from your more average individuals. Explosiveness is that combination of quick reflexes and speed that gets you down the rink faster, gets you away from defenders, and opens up goal-scoring opportunities. How to practice explosiveness? Do what the pros do. Practice the choppy, fast stride that pushes you from a standing start to full speed within seconds. Push off, digging deep, using your legs to stride powerfully. Always practice with a stick in your hand to simulate game conditions.

Skating backward. Hockey is a forward and backward game. Players, no matter what their position, need to be able to skate backward without a care. It's good offense. It's good defense. It's good hockey.

Player Positions

The positions in in-line hockey—forward, defenseman, and goalie (or goaltender)—are the same as with ice hockey, and other than subtleties relating to the two games, there are very few differences in their roles. As a player, you will naturally gravitate to the position that suits your skill level and natural attributes. Are you a fast skater, able to turn quickly and handle the puck well? Then maybe you should be a forward. Quick-reflexed? Then perhaps there's a goalie's position waiting for you.

Forward

Versatility is the watchword for a forward, as this is the individual (actually, individuals) who controls the tempo of the game. The forward plays the entire rink, and to be effective, the individual who aspires to be a top forward should possess outstanding speed and skating skills as well as an ability to see the whole rink. In other words, he should be able to see a play unfolding before it really happens, in order to anticipate the movements of other players and of the puck itself. That means knowing the roles of other players and even developing a knack for sizing opposing players' strengths and weaknesses in order to exploit them during an attack.

The forward is also the playmaker, and he should be able to create and direct plays that will get the puck into the opposing team's end of the rink. That means developing crisp passing skills as well as solid shooting skills. If you're the type of player who enjoys the notion of glory, then forward is the position for you.

Tips for playing forward:
1. *Remember that you represent the concept of offense.* It begins and

Eyes on the puck at all times.

Hockey Rink Dimensions

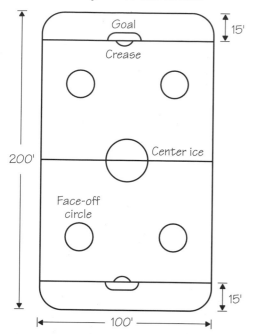

ends with you (usually; sometimes good defensemen become scoring powers, but usually it's the forward), so be proficient at keeping your opponent off balance. Practice puck-handling skills. Learn to shoot. Learn to pass. Do skating drills to improve your ability to turn quickly and speed down the rink (hockey's version of a wind sprint).

2. *Draw the defensman's attention to the puck.* As you come down the rink with the puck, the defenseman will square off and try to take away your offensive options. One way he might do this is by focusing on your body movement as a sign of where you plan to attack. Deflect this observation by a sudden stick move or downward glance that will draw his attention to the puck. Once he begins watching the puck and not you, your job of slipping past him is that much easier.

3. *Don't feel like you have to score to count.* Set up, and be in position for a pass at all times. Be asking yourself where you'll go with the puck if it comes your way. Will you go to the goal? Or will you immediately pass it to another player who has a better angle on the goalie? A tip on passing: Pretend that you're passing eggs back and forth. Push the puck off your stick with a precise wrist movement. Don't slap at it, because you lose the element of control. When receiving a pass, let it come to you. Move your stick backward a few inches as the puck makes its way to you to absorb the shock of puck and stick meeting; that way it won't bounce off and into the hands of another player.

Defenseman

The best defensive players get in the middle of a play as it develops, clogging it up to allow few quality shots on goal. Defensive players are safety valves, so to speak, a line of protection between opposing players and the goalie. The entire job of the defenseman is to align his body with that of the oncoming forward, the shooter. By aligning his body in a way that limits the shooter's scoring options, the defenseman robs the opposing team of an offensive weapon. Further, it's the defenseman's job to get right up into the face of the shooter and rattle him. You want him to be thinking about you, not the shot he's about to take or the pass he's trying to dish off.

The defenseman positions himself to impede the shooter's scoring ability.

Tips for playing solid defense:

1. *Control and adjust your speed to the player coming toward you.* Anticipate where he's going and be there first. It helps to put

yourself into the mind of the shooter. What's he thinking about? Is he setting up to pass off to someone else, or is he planning on taking the shot himself? Is he the sort of shooter who possesses confidence, or will he be easily rattled when you get in his face?

2. *Force the shooter to make the shot from his backhand, or weak, side.* This is done by playing the shooter, using your stick to force him to his backhand by keeping his body to the outside. The less authority that a player is able to shoot with, the more likely he's going to be to rush or push his shot.

3. *Don't make the first move.* You don't know where the offensive player is going, which gives him a slight edge. Counteract this by displaying cagey positioning (see tip 1). You want the shooter to announce his intentions as he approaches the goal. If you make the first move, you may make a mistake and allow the shooter past you (remember, your job is to stay between the shooter and the goal). If the shooter gets past you, the way to prevent a goal from behind is by resorting to a penalty, which you want to avoid at all costs.

4. *Don't watch the puck.* Always, always, always play the body instead of the puck. By keying on a player's body, you'll be able to judge the subtle tics that he may possess that will telegraph his intentions. The puck, however, can be moved around at will by the shooter to throw a defenseman off.

Goalie

By its very definition, the goalie position is synonymous with the mouth of the goal, that last line of defense blocking the other team from scoring. When a team can fool a goalie, it gets past that goalmouth and begins to control the tempo of the game. So to say playing goaltender is a little tense might be an understatement. Good goalies have the ability to deal with the pressure of oncoming players and pucks, knowing how to let the play develop so that they might anticipate from which angle the puck will be flying (or dribbling, or bouncing, or . . .).

Much of in-line hockey is a casual enough game that players can get by with the minimum equipment: pads, helmet, stick, skates. It's not uncommon to see players missing a pad here and there, at least at the street level. (Professional players wear the proper equipment as a matter of course.) However, with goalies, that's different. Even for a casual street game, it's important to have pads covering the extremities. Look into a pair of good hockey pants at your local shop.

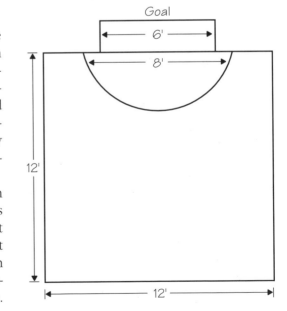

Goal and Crease

They're designed to protect you where it counts. It's also very, very important to have a both a glove and a goalie stick. Sure, they're optional in a very casual game, but to play goalie properly, those pieces of equipment are vital for getting the job done.

Also, and just as important, look into a good mask. Helmets and cages work the best, because they allow a greater field of vision. Believe me, there's nothing like getting a puck off the face to make you rethink any aversion to masks.

Last, get a pair of knee pads. Goalies are forever dropping to their knees to deflect a shot or cover up the goalmouth. That wonderful feeling of bone on rink as you drop to deflect will stay with you for awhile if you don't have the right padding.

Tips for solid goaltending:

1. *Stay in the game mentally.* Much of the time, the play might be happening on the other end of the rink. Sure, it's OK to stand up and lounge against the goal at a time like this, but remember to keep yourself mentally focused and sharp by concentrating on the action. Goaltending is all about focus, and if you drift off, you might be surprised by the long pass that comes your way. Or worse, when the time comes for you to hunker down and

Proper Goalie Form

• Balanced, relaxed position. Able to move quickly in any direction
• Body wide, covering mouth of net
• Eyes focused forward—on the puck

• Stick on the ground, blocking low shots
• Glove hand (left, in drawing) open and ready to catch any airborne puck

block that oncoming shot, you'll be somewhere in la-la land, unable to come back to earth.

2. *Don't commit first.* Like with defensemen, the goalie should force the shooter to make the first move. That goes doubly true for the goalie, though, because if you commit first and get faked out, there's no line of defense to prevent the easy goal. In short, there's no playing catch-up as a goalie. You're either in the goal, blocking the shot, or you're not. Plain and simple.

3. *Cut down the angle.* Don't keep your body inside the goal. Come out a few feet (on a regulation rink, this will coincide with the line marking the top of the crease). You take away the shooter's options when you reduce the angles from which he can take his shot.

4. *Keep the puck frozen as much as possible.* "Freezing" the puck means trapping it in your glove or between your glove and stick in a way that prevents other players from getting to it. The referee will blow "play dead" once you freeze the puck. Play will resume with a face-off, which is good because the action will move away from the mouth of the goal (and you can breathe a sigh of relief) and then perhaps to the other end of the rink.

5. *Work the eyes.* As a player approaches, preparing to make his shot, look him in the eyes to anticipate where his movements will be focused. Very often a player will either stare at, or glance repeatedly toward, the section of the net that he intends to shoot into; or to a player (who might be surreptitiously lurking just out of your field of vision) he intends to pass to. Where most players make their mistake, and where your opportunity to defeat the attack will come about, is by looking down at their stick to make sure the puck is nestled comfortably against the blade. Diffuse the play at that moment by lunging at him and poking your stick into his stick blade. This "poke check" will invariably knock the puck away from him or cause him to lose concentration and get rattled.

How to Shoot the Puck

It's the goal of every player to learn to shoot that blue-line slap shot, the one where you wind up like Gordie Howe and play "old time, Eddie Shore hockey" by smacking the puck from here to eternity. And while you won't get such an opportunity often during a game—that is, if the defense is doing its job right—it's always great to have that weapon in your offensive arsenal.

First, though, it's important to learn the fundamentals of shooting. It's tempting to imagine winding it up and letting it fly on the very first try, but by taking the time to learn the subtle details of what makes a good shot, you'll be better off in the long run. It's important to develop a smooth, fluid shot. That's a process that comes about by learning the basics and by practice, practice, practice. There's no substitute for practice for teaching muscle memory.

Before you shoot, practice good hand position on your stick. Your hands should generally be 1 foot to 1½ feet apart. The top hand should be gripping the bottom of the taped knob atop your stick. The bottom hand should wrap around the stick and form a downward V in the area that the thumb and forefinger grasp the stick. An important point: Hold onto the stick with your fingertips, not with the palm of your hands.

As you move up and down the rink, use the top hand to grasp the stick tightly while using the bottom hand as a guide for flicking passes and other stick-handling skills. However, when it comes time to shoot, tighten the grip of your bottom hand.

The Basic Shot

In order, here's how to shoot the puck:

1. Bend your knees, keeping your stick on the floor at all times.
2. Keep your back straight and your head in position to see the puck and the net at all times.
3. Shift your weight onto your back legs and pull your arms back. Remember to keep your stick on the floor as you set up your shot.
4. Start your shot by shifting your weight from your back leg to your front leg. Don't wind up, but keep that stick cradled against the puck. Winding up, especially when other players are nearby, is the best way to have the puck knocked away. Don't let that happen—protect it.
5. Bring your hands across your body in one fluid motion. Pretend that you're sweeping a broom. Follow through hard and aim at your target with your stick, even after the puck is gone. Note: As in baseball, velocity is increased by increasing stick speed. The faster you sweep those hands through, the faster that puck will travel once you let it fly.

Something that bears emphasizing is the ideal of having control of the puck before you shoot. By slapping at the puck, which happens when the tendency to wind up becomes overwhelming, you lose control. A good hockey player can direct his shot into all corners of the net at will. This skill comes from learning control. You can duplicate it by practicing the fundamentals of control from the very first stages of your shot practice. A typical shot comes off the center of the stick's blade, but better skaters also have developed the ability to have the puck come off the blade in a heel-to-toe fashion in an effort to increase accuracy. Another trick is to change the angle of the stick blade to raise or lower a shot.

When taking a shot during a game, you won't have the luxury (not often, at least) of standing still and lining up your shot. So once you get accomplished enough with the fundamentals of shooting, practice a "game" shot. That is, learn to shoot on the fly. All aspects of the shot will be the same, from bending your knees to maintaining control, but the important aspect will be knowing where you are in relation to the net as you approach the puck. Skate into the puck, then, once your stick is on the ground, proceed with the shot.

A good drill is to line up pucks 10 to 15 feet from the net, then skate back a ways and practice approaching the pucks. Get the feel for skating into the puck, putting your stick down, and shooting. Make sure you maintain control all the way through. Also, make sure you follow through properly by pointing ("aiming" might be a better way to visualize it) your stick at the net after you've shot. I guarantee that if your stick is aimed at the net, then that's where you shot the puck. Very often, a misdirected shot can be traced back to improper follow-through, which happens because the player changes his shot halfway through and doesn't extend the follow-through. The result is a breakdown in aim—and scoring.

Another drill, once you've gotten the hang of the first one, is to include a friend. Have him act as defenseman and try to prevent you from making it to the net. This drill will hone your shooting while simultaneously fostering a stronger competitive drive. Remember, when you shoot, shoot to score, not just get close.

Other Types of Shots

Snap shot. The snap shot is very much like the traditional manner of shooting, but more powerful. Instead of keeping the stick on the ground throughout the shot, however, it's raised slightly before shooting. When making contact it's important to use the combination of forward movement brought on by taking the stick back a few inches) and the snap of your wrist to create a high-speed shot.

Backhand shot. This is a tricky shot, in that the curvature of the stick is away from the puck, thereby taking an element of control away as you shoot. It's not meant to be a long-range shot, but instead a controlled wrist shot that takes place just a few feet from the goal. As the name suggests, this shot originates from your backhand side (the side opposite your natural shooting side). Wayne Gretzky has used the backhand to great effect in ice hockey, sweeping around the backside of the net to score. It's a necessary element of hockey, and something worth perfecting as a means of keeping your opponents off balance.

Slap shot. OK, here it is. If anything, you should learn a great slap shot just to intimidate the opposition. It's a difficult shot to master—as I mentioned, the element of control all but disappears when the stick is raised off the rink—but a dynamic, fun addition to your repertoire. Every player needs to know how to do a slap shot, if for no other reason than it's such a symbol of the game that to actually be a hockey player and not own a slap shot is rather idiosyncratic. I guess goalies are exempt in this respect, but I doubt that a goalie or two hasn't dreamed of parking one in the back of the net from the blue line. Everyone who's ever played hockey has. A hockey player not wanting to fire a slap shot is like a baseball player not wanting to hit a home run.

To learn your very own slap shot, begin by lowering your bottom hand a few inches on your stick. Don't bring it all the way down to the blade, of course, but low enough. Doing so will increase your level of control, making sure that you don't whiff when you swing down on the puck. Nothing like winding up and then missing to make yourself look foolish and to bolster your opponents' confidence. There are various degrees of windup to a slap shot, but for the sake of fun and adventure, let's assume you're trying to learn a full slap shot. This means maximum windup and full power all the way.

The comparison here is golf. To get the maximum amount of power in your slap shot, position the puck just in front of your forward foot, much the same as you would when cranking up for a powerhouse drive on the golf course. Use the same weight transfer technique (weight on the front foot, then on the back foot as you wind up, then back to the front foot as you swing through), then follow through all the way. It goes without saying that you keep your eye on the puck at all times. Also, keep your head down as you swing through to prevent your stick from jerking up involuntarily before striking the puck (end result: the dreaded whiff).

A step-by-step how-to on perfecting a slap shot:
1. Place the puck in front of your forward foot.
2. Begin the windup, drawing your stick as far back as you can.
3. Transfer your weight during the windup from your front foot to your back foot.
4. As you bring your stick down to strike the puck, shift your weight along with it, back toward your front foot.
5. Keep your head down.
6. Follow through by aiming your stick at the net.

Even more than a regular shot, the slap shot will require practice and patience. Gordie Howe didn't learn to wind up and fire away overnight. It takes a while to understand how important control—not power—is when it comes to taking a shot like this. One tip is to start by doing everything in slow motion, the slower the better. You want to teach your muscles to remember the intricate movements involved before you try to speed things up and make the process a whole lot more complex.

Once you get the hang of it, try practicing a game scenario. Skate up the rink, pretending you're all alone: nothing but you and the goalie, one on one. Suddenly, you pull up, rear that mighty stick back, then swat it into the back of the net like it was meant to tear a hole. Imagine the applause of the crowd. Hug your teammates. Notice the dejection on the goalie's face as he glares at the one that got by. Maybe feel sorry for him, even if for just a second. Then go back and practice it again.

I think in-line hockey is a great game, and I think you will, too. It's an especially great sport to teach youngsters, as it teaches those essentials like teamwork and competition and the value of hard work that can sound so much like clichés when used in the abstract, but actually stand for so much. Strangely enough, adults can benefit from the same attributes.

So get out there and give it a try, even if you've never considered yourself a hockey guy (or gal). This is one of those things you'll be glad you tried and one that may stick with you for some time to come.

9
SPEED!

Speed-Skating Basics

Every facet of in-line skating appeals to a certain personality type. Fitness and strength aficionados discover hockey. More aggressive individuals will gravitate toward extreme skating. And for the endurance athletes in the crowd, there's speed skating.

Like in-line hockey, in-line speed skating closely mirrors its ice-bound counterpart. Imagine the low-slung body, aerodynamic grace, and hypnotizing lateral movements of Olympic speed skaters and you'll have some idea of what in-line speed skaters consider good biomechanics. As on the ice, in-line speed skating is deceptive, as the speed can look so effortless while being a physically demanding sport. Also, the ideal of a clearly decided winner—in this case the first person to cross the finish line—carries over.

Feel the need—the need for speed!

But the line blurs. In-line speed skaters don't wear skintight body suits, nor are they limited by the space constraints of a frozen oval. Instead of two-at-a-time racing, as on the ice, in-line speed skaters race in packs. Like Tour de France cyclists, they use their incredible speed to form pace lines and draft off each other. They wear helmets, T-shirts, and Lycra shorts. Top in-line speed skaters race without knee or elbow pads, preferring skin abrasions to the thought of sacrificing speed. But then, not many fall. "I skate as much as I walk. I don't fall down when I'm walking around on my feet," says top speed skater Eddy Matzger, "why should I fall down when I'm skating?" (*Citysports Magazine,* April 1995)

The basics of speed skating are easily understood. The skating motion itself is a series of long, powerful strides that maximize forward movement without sabotaging speed the way that a choppier hockey movement might. Racers maintain a low tuck, bent double at

Note the guy in the hay bales; speed sometimes hurts.

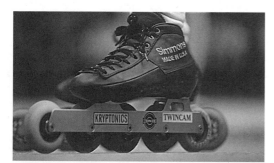

Common and uncommon sights: (Above) Molded leather uppers give the skater more "feel." (Below) A heel brake on a speed skate; note the cable for hand-operation.

the waist, to decrease wind resistance. During long, smooth stretches, the arms are behind the skater, resting on the small of the back to save energy. When extra speed is required, skaters swing their arms from side to side in rhythm with their skating motion to increase momentum and stability.

For those considering competitive speed skating, however, that's not the trick. The trick is to learn the subtle combination of physical fitness and shrewd tactics that makes champions. Knowing how to conserve energy inside the pack can mean the difference between winning and losing.

But maybe competition isn't your aim. Maybe achieving fitness through in-line skating is all you have in mind. If so, then learning to speed skate will help you achieve that objective quicker. The five-wheeled speed skates are more stable than regular skates, but also faster and more demanding. Because of its wide turning radius and singular design (built for speed and nothing else) the speed skate forces the wearer to focus on the dynamics of fitness skating. You will spend more time in an anaerobic state on speed skates, which means you'll burn calories faster and tone muscles to a greater degree. If you like speed—pure, unbridled, effortless speed—and working up a sweat, then speed skating is the way to go.

The Feel of Five Wheels

The first time you slip on a pair of racing boots, you'll notice a big difference between them and other in-line skates. First, they are most often made of leather instead of molded plastic. The leather is designed to mold to the contours of the foot. During a race, this will help the skater detect the slightest nuance that could affect performance, everything from road conditions to the proper alignment of the foot and ankle through a crucial turn. Having a feel for the skate is so important, in fact, that many individuals race without socks to heighten the connection. The idea is that the skate and the foot should feel as one—an extension of the body—thus making all movement somehow flow without effort.

Another difference is boot height. Racing skates reach just above the ankles, instead of rising to midcalf like a recreational skate. The idea is to decrease weight and increase flexibility in order to increase speed. However, the first time most people slip into a racing boot, it feels distinctively wobbly. The muscles and ligaments of the ankle and shin are being forced to support themselves in a manner to which they are unaccustomed. To combat this lack of balance (and as a defense mechanism), the ankles will often bow inward, placing pressure on the inner portion of the wheels. This shift will have a decided impact on speed. With time, however, you will notice the ankles becoming straighter. In turn, your weight will be over the center of the wheels, creating an optimal racing line.

The biggest functional and aesthetic difference between recreational skates and speed skates, however, is the most obvious, and it has nothing to do with the boot. It's the wheels. Speed skates have five wheels instead of four or three, all the better to create a stable platform on which to fly. The fifth wheel extends beyond the front of the foot, easily visible as you peer down from above while skating. The fifth wheel itself doesn't increase speed, but the larger diameter of speed skating wheels does.

In terms of speed, you'll notice the difference the first time you put on your speed skates. It's almost as if they want to start flying immediately. Really, it's that noticeable.

One unfortunate consequence of the fifth wheel is a reduced turning radius. Asking speed skates to make short, snappy turns is akin to asking the same of a freight train—it just doesn't happen. Speed skating turns are wide, carved affairs designed to maintain speed and momentum.

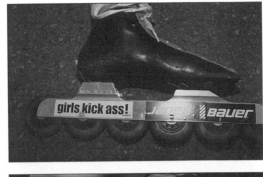

More speed skates

Skating in the Tuck

The speed skating tuck—that low-profile position maintained while racing—is a model of economical motion and focus. Bent double at the waist, the skater quiets the upper body and lets the legs do all the work: push and glide, push and glide, push and glide; long, deliberate strokes that derive their power from the quadriceps, gluteus, and abdominal muscles. A glass of water, it seems, could be balanced without spilling a drop on the skater's horizontal back.

How to develop that tuck? How to learn the sweet synchronicity? It's not easy. Placing the body low to the ground with the arms pinned behind the back feels grossly unnatural. In fact, when tried for the first time, it feels extremely perilous. The natural inclination is to stand straighter, keep those arms shoulder-width apart—maintain a perfect balance, one in which recovery from near falls will be automatic.

But balance isn't the point, speed is. Fledgling speed skaters must learn to skate in the tuck if their aim is to be champions. It's just part of the game. The weird part is that by developing the ability

High-speed skating can be a blur.

Proper Speed-Skating Form

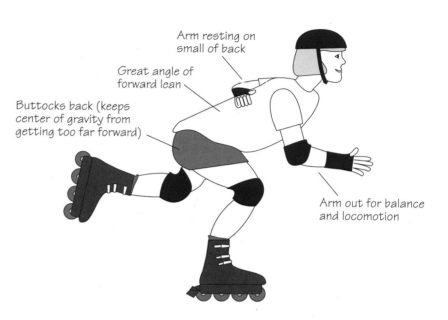

Arm resting on
small of back

Great angle of
forward lean

Buttocks back (keeps
center of gravity from
getting too far forward)

Arm out for balance
and locomotion

to skate in the tuck, the skater vastly improves balance and coordination. Suddenly, the idea of using leather boots to increase a feel for the skate and the road becomes apparent as well. The skater needs to be sensate from head to toe, a dialed-in speed machine whose sole focus is moving forward, always forward.

To learn the tuck, it's best just to take your speed skates out of the box and learn to skate easily in them for a few days. Adjust to the greater speed of five wheels. Learn to turn. A good drill to learn agility and a feel for the skates is to play soccer on the street with a few friends—wearing your skates. The idea is to become light on your feet and able to anticipate how your skates will respond in a variety of situations ranging from sudden stops to lateral leaps to impromptu bursts of speed as you chase the ball. Sounds weird, but it works. Another drill is to play tag. Again, acceleration, bursts of lateral movement, sudden hesitations—perfect for getting to know balance.

As you develop a comfort level on speed skates, find a quiet stretch of pavement where you can practice your tuck. While pushing and gliding, begin bending slowly at the waist as if taking a bow. Thrust your butt back as if you're about to sit in a chair, keep your knees bent, and maintain your center of gravity directly over your skates: too far back and you'll lose speed, too far forward and you'll feel as if you're about to pitch onto your chin. Swing your arms from side to side, then slowly quiet them by placing them first on the hips, then on the small of the back. (Despite the aerodynamic benefits of this latter location, some racers still prefer to rest them on the hips. Either way, it's a matter of personal comfort.)

Most people don't get the hang of it right away. It takes awhile before the body relaxes and gets in tune with the skates enough for you to feel totally comfortable in the tuck position. Every self-preservatory fiber within the body must be retrained to believe that lowering the center of gravity and placing the arms behind your back is not a surefire prescription for disaster. Unfortunately, the racing tuck is a full-commitment position—either you're in it or you're not. A half-tuck is an extremely ineffective way to increase speed, so don't allow yourself to stop learning until you're able to lower yourself all the way.

The biggest deterrent to learning the tuck is a fear of falling. Combat this by distracting yourself. Try this thirty-minute drill: skate for ten minutes without moving your upper body. It's easier if your keep both hands behind your back. This will force your legs to do all the work of maintaining equilibrium. Skate for ten more minutes, this time in a half-squat, with your rear end thrust out as if you were about to sit down in a chair. Feel that? It's your quadriceps screaming at you. They want relief. Give it to them by leaning your torso forward for the final ten minutes of the drill. Remove one arm from the small of your back to use for balance as necessary. It's not necessary to get your back parallel with the ground—yet—merely bend forward as far as comfort will allow. The burning sensation in your upper legs will disappear immediately as the impetus for maintaining balance shifts to the abdominal muscles. What's more, now that your body has grown accustomed to skating without the upper body as a balancing tool, it will actually thank you for leaning forward.

Once you've learned the tuck, come back to your quiet stretch of pavement as often as possible to practice the position again and again. Practice until it becomes second nature. You'll find that once you get comfortable hunkered down over the toe of your skate, face seemingly skimming off the pavement, that standing up straight while skating feels very slow by comparison.

A few things to think about to maximize speed:
1. At full extension, the pushing skate should always be in front of the gliding skate.

2. Drive equally with both legs. Most people favor one leg or the other, so they make it their "power" leg, relying on it for power to the detriment of the other leg. Be cognizant of this tendency and avoid it.

3. Look for your personal "balance point" as you skate. This is the perfect alignment of body and skate that allows effortless skating. You'll know you've found it when you don't have to tense the supporting muscles of the foot, ankle, and shin to correct imbalances. Find it for straightaways, then again for turns.

Strength in Numbers

Once you've mastered the tuck, it doesn't mean it's time to hop into a race. There's the small matter of other skaters to consider. Skating alone leaves a wide margin for error. Skating with a pack does not. To preclude being overwhelmed when you step to the starting line for your first race, it's vitally important that you find a local skating club or just a handful of buddies and learn the quiet thrill of skating in a pack.

More so than most any bit of advice in this book, there's an unspoken etiquette to pack skating that must be experienced in order to be fully understood. You must learn to be comfortable with other skaters in front, behind, and to both sides of you. You must learn to go with the flow as the pack rounds a turn en masse, each wheel following the same invisible arc. If worse comes to worst, you must also learn how to dodge fallen skaters or crash without injuring yourself.

The only way to get comfortable with these sensations is by practicing with a group. It will heighten your level of awareness, increase your use of peripheral vision, and, above all, decrease your fear of packs. This, in turn, will relax you. Tense skaters are less likely to react properly in a tight situation.

While learning, there's no need to bring a high level of organization to your group skates. Get in the habit of skating as a loose bunch. This should be fun skating, nothing else. You'll develop a feel for the amount of room you'll need between yourself and others so that neither wheels nor arms nor legs collide.

Drafting

To skate behind another individual so closely that he or she substantially decreases the amount of wind you must battle is known as drafting. It is not cheating, but rather an accepted method of conserving energy during a race, particularly on blustery days (proper etiquette is for all skaters to take turns being the individual at the front of this line, called a pace line).

Once you've gotten comfortable skating in a pack, organize the same group of friends into a single-file line. In the tuck position, practice skating in a line. Allow 2 to 3 feet between yourself and the skater in front of you. Try to synchronize your hand and leg movements with that skater's. As a test, step to the side—out of the draft—and feel how the sudden addition of wind forces you to work harder. Stepping back into the line, practice staying in the draft again. Remember to always be aware of your surroundings. Know where cars and curbs are at all times. Lift your head up from time to time (but don't stand upright—the sudden wind resistance will slow you way down and force individuals behind you to slam into your backside) and make yourself aware of road conditions like potholes, gravel, and pieces of debris.

When it's your turn to take position at the front, be cognizant that setting the pace is now your responsibility: too fast and you risk breaking up the pack, as there may be some individuals who won't be able to keep up (while this is perfect strategy in a race, it may cost you a few training partners); too slow and the group will suddenly lose rhythm. You'll have wheels on your heels and hear the sudden yelp of your buddies telling you to pick up the pace, another surefire way to lose training partners.

Pace lines are fragile units of momentum. Skaters naturally feel more comfortable with those who do as little as possible to upset the synchronicity of the pace line, as they know that this is how skating enjoyment is heightened and crashes are kept to a minimum. Teach yourself to be cognizant of pace and pacing at all times.

A good example of drafting. The guy up front is doing all the work. The guy in back just goes along for the ride.

Breaking Away

Here we have the opposite of drafting. A breakaway is when the leader—sometimes accompanied by a few capable friends—sprints away from the pace line to become a separate entity. There's a bit of work involved here, as those within the confines of the pace line are enjoying the resting benefits of letting other individuals break the wind. The breakaway group not only has to summon the energy to drop the pack, but they have to find the power to do it decisively as well. Breakaways fail all the time because the defectors were physically and mentally unable to convince themselves and the pack that they were capable of dropping them.

Breakaway!

So lets say that you're skating up front, letting a pace line of buddies or competitors draft off of you. You feel the wind in your face, you feel the mental strain of trying to find just the right tempo, you feel your lungs and legs working harder than they did inside the pace line. Suddenly, you sense two things: a burst of strength signaling that your body is capable of going faster without much more effort, and a weakness in the pack—they're having a hard time keeping up. Strategically, that is when you go.

The common denominator in breakaways is the element of surprise. This isn't the kind of thing where you turn around and invite a half-dozen friends along. You just go, and you go decisively. Using both arms for momentum, sprint away from the pack. Think of it as an attack. Don't hold back. Push yourself beyond your personal redline. The pack will gobble you up and stifle that breakaway easily if you don't speed away with all you're worth. Remember, your goal is to put physical distance between you and the pack. Without being paranoid, it's not stretching the imagination for you to pretend they're all out to get you and that you must get away as quickly as you can, because that's exactly what they're doing.

One of three things will happen after you break away:
1. It will be such a meager, slipshod breakaway that you'll quickly be caught by the pack.
2. Three or four others will "read" your breakaway before it happens. Anticipating your sudden sprint, they'll go with you. This is a good thing. The group will form a new, smaller pace line and help each other sustain the breakaway. (Of course, you'll have to deal with them sometime between the breakaway and the finish line, but that's a matter for a separate breakaway.)
3. The pack will stutter collectively and you'll whistle away from them like their worst fear. If they hesitate, take advantage and push even harder. Sometimes a pack won't chase down a breakaway because they believe the skater is unable to pull it off. If that's the case, try with all your might to prove them wrong.

Breakaways are heart-thumping gambles. You can practice them (alone, preferably—no sense in letting the world know about this new weapon in your arsenal) by throwing sudden, violent 100-meter sprints into your regular training runs. Instead of resting after the sprint, force yourself to resume your prior pace. This is how it will feel during a race. Remember that as the body trains, so the body races.

Interval Workouts and Other Agonies

Which brings us to conditioning. Other than better equipment, two things will make you a faster skater: proper technique and conditioning. We've discussed technique, so let's take a look at conditioning. Ideally, speed skaters should train a little like distance runners. That means endurance-building workouts, pacing workouts, and speed workouts.

Endurance-building sessions. These are long, slow skates of an hour or more that are typically done in the early part of a training cycle. The purpose is to get the mental feel of going the distance and to train the body (especially heart, lungs, circulatory system, and excretory system) to be comfortable performing for long periods of time. It's important to do these at "conversation pace" (defined as the ability to talk effortlessly and skate at the same time). You'll notice an ability to go farther with less effort after a few months of these.

Pacing workouts. Every race takes place at a certain average speed. It's higher for elite skaters, lower for beginning skaters. This is known as *race pace,* and for you to race competently it's important to know beforehand what this feels like. Many new racers make the mistake of doing nothing but endurance-building skates before a big race, then wonder why they feel out of breath and tire so quickly once the race begins. It's because they've trained their body to go long and slow. Races are fast, and the body must learn to thrive in the state of oxygen depletion that occurs during a race. Remember, as the body trains, so the body races.

Once you've built up endurance, teach your body to feel comfortable at race pace. A curious thing about physiology is that the body gets stronger during a state of rest *after being stressed* (this last emphasis to discourage the recliner set from refraining even further from physical activity). So when doing race pace work, it's important to break it up with rest. A typical workout might go something like this: Warm up with a twenty-minute skate; skate five minutes at race pace, then rest by skating easily for five minutes (repeat this "five on, five off" scenario several times); cool down with ten easy minutes.

Speed workouts. This is where you teach your body to sprint. You need this ability to get off the line fast at the start of a race, you need it for breakaways, and you need it for your end-of-the-race "kick." Teach your body to unleash speed instead of forcing it out. Try this workout: After warming up, perform a set of ten 200-meter sprints. Instead of straining, begin each sprint easily. Force yourself to relax as you slowly pick up the pace in the first 20 meters. You'll find that by relaxing, your body will get comfortable with the idea of all-out speed. Let it go, let it flow.

A Few Words on Speed for Noncompetitors

Even noncompetitors can benefit from dabbling in speed skating. The increased speed, lower boot, and lack of braking heighten awareness of skating fundamentals. Even if you're not planning on purchasing a pair of in-line speed skates, many fundamentals of speed skating can be practiced on four-wheel in-lines—to your benefit.

There's something about finding an open stretch of asphalt and letting loose the inner need for speed that I find eternally invigorating. Unbridled speed is so contrary to the lazy push and glide often associated with in-lining that the change of pace can seem almost heretical. Maybe it has something to do with pushing personal limits, but if you take the opportunity to work on speed—just speed—one day of every week, you'll find slower speeds just that much easier to deal with as your ability to react to problem circumstances (road hazards, quick stops, off-balance recovery) at speed becomes second nature. Again, that translates into greater relaxation; greater relaxation translates into greater control.

10

EXTREME SKATING

In-lining is a sport that seems to have found itself capable of expanding in ways that defy description. How else can you explain a sport that started as no more than a dry-land training device for ice skaters but now features people grinding the frames of their skates along walkway railings, leaping off steps and over cars, or even doing back flips on vertical sections of ramp?

That's not all. Couples regularly buckle their skates on and dance around like Fred Astaire and Ginger Rogers as part of in-line skate dancing. There's also in-line figure skating, which is very similar to Olympic figure skating.

Let's start off by exploring extreme skating, which—along with recreational skating, hockey, and speed skating—is considered one of the sport's four most identifiable subdivisions. Extreme skating actually got its start back in the mid-1970s, when skateboarders began using urethane on wheels instead of steel or clay. They found that they could skate on vertical surfaces, such as empty swimming pools or homemade plywood ramps, and at first, that was a feat in and of itself.

But soon the mere act of skating on vertical was overshadowed by those individuals who learned to launch themselves up and out of the pool or ramp, then grab the rail of their board and guide it safely through a turn and back onto the ramp. "Pulling air" became the defining characteristic of skating on vertical, and the more extreme the air, the better.

Soon, roller skaters began trying it. There was no love lost between the skateboarders, who considered themselves purists (and territorial—the locations of ramps and pools were preciously

Catching air above the half-pipe

More air

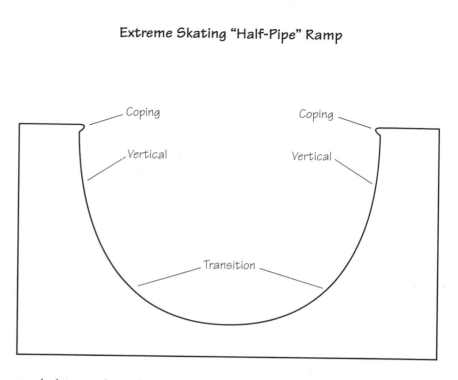

Extreme Skating "Half-Pipe" Ramp

Coping

Vertical

Coping

Vertical

Transition

guarded secrets), and it wasn't uncommon for roller skaters to report getting spit on or beat up in pursuit of their new hobby. On a more macho level, there was also an inference by skateboarders that the roller skaters were less than manly, which made no sense whatsoever because the roller skaters didn't have the option of bailing out when the going got rough. Unlike skateboarders, they were securely bound to their wheels, and they often paid the price for it. (Most of the skateboarders and roller skaters who first tried the extreme stuff were guys.)

So it's a wonder that the concept of skating on vertical while wearing wheels lasted long enough to see the advent of in-lines. It did, though, and now the mere act of pulling air is a stepping-off point for the outrageous stunts that are being performed. There are back flips and somersaults and fakie air (riding backward up the ramp and somersaulting to land face first). There's inverted air, where the skater does a handstand on the side of the ramp in the course of pulling air.

The extreme side of in-line skating has attracted a hard-core audience that feels prepared to offer their bodies up in the pursuit of new moves. Mostly younger, they will go to great lengths to try something new (though you'll never hear them use the word *dangerous*).

Going to the Extreme

How to go about becoming an extreme skater? It's a matter of proficiency first. The skater must be good enough to do simple things like leaping in the air or leaping off curbs before moving on to the more outrageous avenues. The best extreme skaters tend to wear their skates almost everywhere they go, because there's always the opportunity that they could come across a new obstacle to challenge ("Let's jump down that flight of stairs!") and in turn bring about decided growth in skating prowess. When you wear your skates everywhere, they become part of your personality and an extension of your legs. I would recommend that anyone serious about pursuing extreme in-line skating take that attitude about skating. The matter goes even further than a mere increase in proficiency. Extreme skating is a total-commitment state of mind. Those who are serious about it dedicate themselves to it in a total-commitment way, and if that means wearing skates everywhere they go, then they wear skates everywhere they go.

I'm not going to go into the tricks or moves in this book. Tricks change quickly, and both the types and the names of the moves are usually outdated by the time a book like this is more than a year old. Instead, I urge you to go back and work on some of the basics: turning, proper balance, center of gravity, skating backward, and so on. Once you've mastered these, seek out other extreme skaters and learn the moves and terminology from them. You'll find them almost everywhere.

If you live near a large city, chances are the National In-Line Skate Series (NISS) will be coming your way during the summer months. Most major in-line magazines (see the appendix) will have information about these competitions. They're a great way to watch top skaters and learn the moves that seem like they'll be perfect for you.

Hard landings are a part of the game.

Half-pipes can fit anywhere—even in a backyard.

11

CROSS-TRAINING:

Using Skating to Train for Other Sports

In-lining, while a form of fitness in and of itself, can also serve a useful purpose for those who have achieved a degree of proficiency—namely, to help you train for other sports. We've already discussed the specific muscles and muscle groups worked by in-lining. Now it's time to apply that new strength in a way that will benefit your performance in other arenas. The term for this overlapping of skills is known as *cross-training.*

Cross-training with in-lines will increase strength and endurance, help your body recover from tough workouts, and give you a mental break for those days when you would rather go out and have fun than engage in a strenuous workout. It's the perfect sport for those days when you want a workout that feels "effortless" while at the same time you know that your body could benefit from a touch of exertion. In short, when you want to put a little fun in your run, put on those skates.

Cycling is one sport that benefits from in-line cross-training.

Cross-Training's Effect on Muscle Memory

Before launching into specifics, remember that the same path toward *muscle memory* (defined as a series of movements repeated so frequently that the body performs them without effort) that made in-lining second nature can also work against you when it comes to cross-training. Remember—and this holds especially true if you are the sort of athlete who has been involved with other sports for a long period of time—you've also got muscle memory for other sports.

Running, for instance, is a series of tiny movements—foot strike, push-off, arm swing, body motion—that have become ingrained, and in-lining will in no way affect your ability to perform those movements. But within each of these running movements are minute subcomponents such as angle of heel strike, whether you supinate or pronate as you roll your foot during its time on the ground, and whether you push off with the inside or outside parts of your toes during each footfall.

A downside of cross-training with in-lines is that it can change these minute subcomponents (with adverse affects) by subtly rewiring muscle memory. When running, instead of pushing off with your toes, you might find yourself sweeping your leg out and away from your body just as you do when in-line skating. (I once watched the hockey team at Northern Michigan University do conditioning work by running laps on the college track. It was like watching ducks try to run. But put those same guys on skates and they were fluid and graceful.)

The end result is that you might become a lesser runner while becoming a better skater, or that you might find your running motion changed in a way that brings about injury. For instance, a friend of mine used in-lining exclusively to recover from a knee injury. When he went back to running, he found a certain awkwardness to his stride, as if he were waddling. With a bit of thinking, he pinpointed the reason: muscle memory aspects of in-lining—in his case, the rotation of the hips during the push and glide—had changed his running form. With a bit of work, he finally fixed the problem.

Why does this short-circuit of muscle memory happen? Because everyone's body has a certain, unique way of performing an exercise movement, done in such a way as to increase efficiency and decrease the risk of injury. So beware the subtle changes brought on by muscle memory alterations from too much cross-training. It can lead to injury and reduce your enjoyment of those other sports until you "rewire" that portion of your brain dealing with muscle memory once again—in the other direction.

This discussion isn't meant to scare you away from cross-training. The foregoing paragraph is something of a disclaimer, to prevent inadvertent injury and to remind you that the key to successful training is balance, whether it be in time spent training or in the percentage of time spent practicing various sports. Cross-training, whether with in-lines, with weights, in a game of basketball, or all of the above, is meant as a supplement to—not a replacement for—whatever sport you're training for. For instance, if you plan on running a marathon, you're making a mistake if you train solely by in-lining (don't laugh;

I've seen it done). You may finish the marathon, but not as quickly as if you'd trained by running a great percentage of the time, then used in-lining on recovery days and to increase strength.

And always, no matter what you're training for, train in moderation. The body gets strong during the rest (also known as the *recovery* phase) of a training cycle, not through the act of exercise, which is the process of tearing the body down so that it might rebuild itself. If you train day after day without rest, always trying to push yourself to go harder and faster, then you need to think of using in-lines one or two days a week, if for no other reason than to allow your body a chance to recover. You will see performance improvement almost immediately.

Here are just a few sports you can cross-train for with in-line skates.

Downhill Skiing

All skiers know the fundamentals behind carving a turn: weighting and unweighting, using the inside edge of the outside ski, maintaining the center of gravity, keeping skis parallel. Well, with a few variations, the same can be said of in-line skating. A great many skiers use in-lines as a dry-land training substitute for that very reason. Very strong skaters go one step further, using downhill sections of pavement and rubber-tipped ski poles to closer approximate the sensation of skiing. Less adventurous skaters enjoy zipping along flatland, imagining themselves weighting and unweighting inside edges on an Aspen slope.

What's the best way to use in-lining to improve your skiing? Here are a few ideas. A good rule of thumb, no matter what you do, is to keep a strong mental image of yourself on skis. This bit of imagery will take you away and help you focus on skiing mechanics. It might help that ski boots and in-line skates have a very similar fit and dynamic.

Turning fundamentals. These can be done on either flatland or a slope, with or without poles. With a little speed, practice making turns as if you were on a ski slope: Keep your upper body still, with your chest pointed down an imaginary fall line. In the absence of edges, simulate putting pressure on the inside edge as you turn by using your toes and arch to put pressure on the inside of your boot. Remember, this is done with the outside foot (i.e., during a left turn, it would be the right boot; during a right turn, the left).

To avoid letting your inside boot (the one not carving the turn) detract from a smooth, fluid turn, either lift that foot off the ground entirely or make sure that it just skims the ground. Just as in skiing, a poorly placed inside boot can cause a crash (usually by causing the tips to cross). Be careful not to place your weight on the wrong foot during a turn.

Arc long lazy turns, then slowly tighten them until they're tight. Focus on shifting weight from skate to skate as you come out of each turn. A poorly carved turn will cause a skid. Focus on keeping your weight centered—not too far back, where it's over the heels, nor too far forward, where you'll notice the balls of your feet trying to grip the inner boot for purchase.

Slalom. The idea here is to practice short, snappy turns and to keep the upper body focused straight ahead. Set up an imaginary course. As you make each turn, emphasize that your shoulders are always parallel to the ground while your hips and ankles sway beneath you. These are your pivot points. The minute you start dipping and swaying your shoulder with each turn, the sooner your turns will become sloppy and disparate. Keep your eyes focused well in front of you instead of down at the ground.

Remember, don't use your knees to pivot. Knees lack a great deal of lateral movement (read: none) and are notorious for becoming injury prone when torqued. Avoid this possibility by using ankles and hips for pivoting and knees for leaning forward and back.

Cross-Country Skiing

There are two different styles of cross-country skiing. There's traditional Nordic skiing, which involves the well-known kick-and-glide movement. Then there's the newer variation, skating. Let's deal with the latter first.

Skating. Each movement, with the exception of using poles, is exactly like in-line skating. Instead of kick and glide, it copies in-line push and glide. On uphills, the herringbone method (ski tips out, weight on inside edges) is used as a source of locomotion. On downhills, the skis are parallel and gravity does the work. Even more than downhill skiing, the skating style of Nordic skiing is similar to in-lining. It makes a perfect off-season cross-training tool and a great form of mental relaxation. For those in-line skaters living in parts of the country where snow and ice are synonymous with winter, the skating style of cross-country skiing is a perfect winter substitute.

Traditional Nordic skiing. The push-and-glide movement has been copied on dry land for years by hard-core skiers through the use of roller skis. These short cross-country skis mounted on wheels offer a great form of wheeled training. However, in-lining can be just as effective. Start by purchasing a pair of rubber-tipped poles. Bring these with you as you skate. Use them to build upper body strength by keeping your legs quiet and using your arms in a "double pole" fashion, that is, using the poles in sync. Or try skating a long uphill, pointing your skates outward in the herringbone style and using your poles to make the job easier.

Running

Recovery days. The day after a tough running workout, give your legs a break from the pounding. Slip into your skates and skate slowly for a half hour. It will help your body flush the lactic acid by-products from your system and speed recovery. *Active recovery*, as this training technique is known, still gives you a workout, but without the stressors generally associated with breakdown.

Hard days. In lieu of going for a short, fast run, try blasting a few miles in your in-lines. Studies have shown that you'll be able to get your heart rate up almost as high on in-lines as you would during a regular run. Though the push and glide doesn't simulate the running motion perfectly, it does place an emphasis on the glutes and quadriceps, two muscles runners notoriously leave underdeveloped. Why bother building those muscles? They're the ones you'll call on to power you through a tough series of hills.

This runner wears a heart-rate monitor to gauge hard and easy efforts.

Cycling

Strength and Endurance. Because the low-profile in-line stance is similar to the position of a cyclist down on the drops (the lower portion of racing handlebars), and because the legs are slightly behind the torso while pushing, skating is perfect for cyclists.

Hill repeats. Build quadricep and gluteus strength by doing hill intervals on your in-lines. Starting at the base of a 200-meter hill, sprint as hard as you can for the first 50 yards to develop momentum, then settle into a push and glide as best you can. As your speed from the initial sprint drains off, feel the quadriceps work to push you up the hill. Exaggerate the push stroke to make the glutes work harder. Use your arms—both of them, as now is not the time for

Hill repeats hurt—but they work.

For the feel of life beyond pavement, try out your powerful new in-line legs on a mountain bike.

your upper body to be quiet—to gain new momentum. You'll go anaerobic (into oxygen debt) almost immediately, and you will stay that way to the top of the hill. Rest once you get there, then slowly skate back down. Repeat to exhaustion.

Tennis

Tennis is a game of quick starts and stops, both forward and lateral. As in skating, the legs do almost all the work. Although a series of lateral jumps on your skates can be tricky, when done properly there is little reason to fear falling. In fact, to prove this is not an entirely unnatural motion for skaters, watch hockey players sometime and note how easily they move laterally on their skates.

The first cross-training exercise, then, is lateral movement. Starting on a smooth, level, wide stretch of blacktop, stand with your skates parallel and shoulder-width. Pretend you are a tennis player at the baseline and can only range left and right across the expanse, never forward. In short bursts, practice scuttling five yards to the left of your starting point, then five yards back. Then go five yards right and back. Make sure to keep your weight centered as you move back and forth, back and forth. Pick up the tempo as you get used to the feeling. If you can, push yourself to a state of oxygen-debt, so that your body experiences the same fatigued and winded state it experiences in a lengthy baseline rally. You should feel your muscles start to burn from the effort, especially in the inner and outer thigh (adductor and abductor). Notice how keeping your body loose but upright helps you move faster and with more control than when you hunch over too far at the waist.

Stop after a minute. Check your pulse. Rest until your pulse rate falls to 120. Then start again, going for another minute. Repeat this process of exertion and rest five times if you're doing it exercise for the first time, ten times if you've tried it before.

Here's another way to build tennis speed. Instead of improving baseline movement, this one's a surefire way to help increase your leg speed as you charge the net. On that same expanse of blacktop, set up a course 50 meters long and at least 10 meters wide (just to give yourself some elbow room). Beginning at one end, sprint the 50 meters, turn around, then sprint back without allowing yourself any rest beyond the turnaround. Repeat ten times.

Next, do a series of lateral right and left quicksteps on your skates, then sprint those same 50 meters. Again, turn around quickly and line up to start. Step right, step left, then sprint 50 meters. As in soccer, this is a combination of lateral movement and forward acceleration, combined with a lung-busting lack of rest.

The number of sports that benefit from in-line cross-training, as you can see, are numerous. In-lining is that rare sport that combines strength and endurance in a package entirely devoid of drudgery. Compare, for instance, cross-training on a stair machine or treadmill to the joy of in-lines. Doesn't it sound rather tame and boring by comparison?

Use your imagination to come up with new ways of cross-training on your in-lines. Always avoid exercises that place excess torque on the knees. And since some of these exercises involve high rates of speed or backward skating, please make sure to avoid areas where a crash is possible. The same goes with downhill and uphill skating, because that usually involves a road or parking garage of some sort.

Have fun getting fitter.

12

BRINGING UP BABY

Ah, childhood. It was a time when everything was simple, at least in memory. For many people, childhood was when they first skated, clipping a bulky pair of metal roller skates (with clay wheels) to their Keds and skittering off down the sidewalk. There were no pads then, so skinned knees were commonplace. (Funny how no kids I knew ever smacked their head skating, despite all those injury figures that show head traumas as occurring in over 10 percent of all crashes.)

Anyway, we were skating down the sidewalk. Maybe you had a lemonade stand going at the same time. Maybe it was a hot summer day (probably, because not everyone grows up in California). As standard as those memories may sound—almost a Norman Rockwell take on childhood and skating—there is almost definitely one part you don't remember about skating and childhood: your parents. There was little or no roller skating for adults, other than the occasional night out at the local rink. All that has changed, however, and generations who grew up before the advent of Rollerblades will be the last to be able to say that they can't recall seeing an adult on skates.

Let's face it, nowadays almost as many adults buy skates for themselves as for their kids. Accordingly, the adults of the in-line era are the first with the privilege of skating alongside their kids as they learn. In effect, the child is learning by watching Mom and Dad. It becomes a family adventure.

No fear.

Skating with Children

There are several great reasons you should buy in-line skates for your kids. First, in-line skating develops balance and coordination, which in turn develop self-confidence. Second, the repetitive nature of practicing skating will instill in your child a feel for perseverance and dedication, two traits that will come in handy in life (like the old saying goes, perseverance builds character). Third, in-line skating is fast becoming one of the most popular forms of recreation for children. Remember, sales figures published by the National Sporting Goods Association in July 1995 showed that sales of in-line gear were roughly parallel that of Little League baseball equipment. Not that in-line is about to replace baseball as the national pastime, but when a sport is that popular among kids, it can only serve to build their self-esteem if they are competent at that sport.

In short, in-line is popular, an arena for character building, and a great medium for developing physical fitness within kids. Those are good things, no doubt about it. It's also a good bet that the child who can skate well has a good sense of self-esteem. It's just that kind of sport.

So what are the drawbacks of putting your kid in skates? One word: injuries. It would be ludicrous to deny that the possibility exists. Worse, it would be ludicrous not to mention it in a book like this. I have two children, and though they are great skaters, I still hear little alarm bells going off in my head when they crash.

Whenever people begin discussing in-line phobias, the number one reason for not giving it a try is fear of injury. Broken bones, chipped teeth, fractured skulls, the list is seemingly exhaustive. Those fears are doubled when it concerns your child. What parents want to see their child injured in any way? Fortunately, as we've already discussed, the protective gear available now makes falling a relatively painless experience. By wearing a helmet, slipping on knee and elbow pads, and making sure to wear supportive wrist protection, the chances of your child having a negative skating experience are minimal.

Having said all that, there's no reason not to teach your children all about the sport and to make in-lining a family experience. Your kids are probably already planting subtle hints about their desire for a brand-new pair of skates anyway, so you might as well teach them.

What, you say? Me? Teach? Yes, you. By now you have become quite the in-line pro, able to leap off ramps (well, maybe), speed down hills in a tuck, and slalom through traffic on your local in-line rink. The same sport that has brought you fitness and the perception of increased coordination is there for your kids to learn. They will love it because it's cool and because it's fun. You will love it because you can spend a little extra time with your kids.

So how do you teach your child?

Teaching Junior to Skate

Lets backtrack. Remember where I said that you're a pro now? Well, I was being facetious, and it is important that you recognize that. Whether or not you are able to make magic with your skates is of no consequence when it comes to teaching kids. In fact, the worst possible thing you can do is to wait until you feel like an expert before teaching your child to skate. Why? Because that day, for one reason or another, may never come.

Try to remember simply that you are confident in skates. That's what your child—or any pupil, for that matter—will pick up. If you are confident and relaxed in your skates, the feeling will be contagious. If it helps at all, try to remember that children learn to skate more quickly than adults do. They're not as worried about looking foolish, and they have a greater amount of flexibility, which results in fewer injuries when they do fall. So if you have not quite achieved the level of competence you had hoped to attain, remember that practicing with your children—for whom falling and looking foolish is no big deal—will make you a better skater. Their enthusiasm will make you more relaxed. If anything, practicing with your children and watching them skate will get you down the road to expert a lot faster than going it alone will.

There are a few things to keep in mind as you prepare your child for in-lining. First, not all children are ready for full-fledged in-lines. Bear in mind that if your child is very young (less than four), it might be better to start the tot off with "toy" in-lines. These slip on over the child's shoe, come up above the ankle, and have wide rollers instead of wheels. They do not go very fast (in fact, they barely move) and serve no purpose other than to allow your child to feel comfortable on skates. Instead of trying to balance on wobbly, narrow wheels, the toddler merely has to contend with the unusual sensation of rolling forward uncontrollably. (When I first began skating, I wished that such a convenience existed for adults.)

Second, when teaching a child to skate, your physical presence by your youngster's side can be more reassuring than the world's

When skating with very young children, always stay close enough to lend a hand.

Toy skates: a great place to start. Note the middle wheel that slides laterally to create a more stable platform.

best pair of pads. This holds especially true with small children, who have a less confident sense of balance. I suggest that until the youngster gets a feel for the skates and the sensation of movement, take your own skates off and hold his or her hand while walking alongside as the child skates. Once your child develops an ease atop skates and is not afraid of rolling forward (*afraid* is perhaps the wrong word to describe children's reactions to their first time on skates; it is merely disorientation, which can lead to panic), put your in-lines on and skate behind the child. Keep your skates to the outside of the child's, supporting her or him by the hips or under the shoulders. Do a snowplow as you skate forward to keep speed from building too quickly or going out of control. Soon your child will tell you, "I'd rather try it alone," which is the first step toward competence, then graduation into regular in-line skates.

One note about "toy" in-lines: Because they're made to be worn over shoes, the buckling system is often looser than it should be, which creates a lack of ankle, shin, and foot support. While children are more flexible than adults, there is the danger of injury if the buckles aren't tightened to maximum snugness.

Skating for Safety

As when teaching a child to ride a bike, one of the greatest responsibilities facing a parent with in-line instruction is imbuing the rules of the road within children. Instead of looking at roads and parking lots as neatly segmented, subdivided, and otherwise partitioned, children look at those great expanses and see nothing but an asphalt playground. Teach them to recognize the specifics of street behavior and to follow these rules:

1. On a road, always skate on the sidewalk. If there is no sidewalk, stay to the left, facing traffic.
2. Practice the buddy system. Children skating alone are hard for drivers to see. Have children pair up when skating and be each other's eyes and ears, always on the lookout for cars, bicycles, pedestrians, and other skaters.
3. Cross the street only at crosswalks.
4. Avoid in-lining in parking lots. Drivers backing out or pulling in have a difficult time spotting a fast-moving skater.
5. Always wear safety gear, especially a helmet.

Real In-Lines

The first time a child moves up from "toy" skates to regular in-lines is a great opportunity to acquaint them with the aforementioned safety rules. These rules should be further reinforced through daily reminders.

When children move up to real in-lines, it's best to begin as you did: by sitting them down and showing them a little about the inner workings of their new pair of in-lines. It's not necessary to slip the inner boot out and give a detailed lecture about skate construction. But it won't tax your children too much—and may even save a great deal confusion down the road—if you explain the significance of the inner boot (insulation, padding). Take a few minutes and walk through the workings of the buckles or laces. Point out how the wheels are situated and the importance of preventing rocks or other bits of debris from getting lodged between the wheels and the frame. Explain what bearings are, and point out that the sound of a worn bearing is just that: a sound. Remember, a new bearing should make no sound whatsoever.

Help your children put their skates on. Then help them to their feet. Make sure to support them by either walking alongside them or skating behind them. As they experience the effortless joy of push and glide on their own, you might find a perverse thrill in noting that your children are going through the same awkward learning experience you enjoyed so thoroughly (it's a bonding experience). The ankles will bow in, the wheels will feel uncontrollable, turning will be a heretical thought, stopping will seem the impossible dream. Encourage the kids by telling them that you went through the same experience. That will bolster their confidence if they are having a tough go of it.

Let them know that in-line skating is not something that comes naturally to many people and that falling down (they'll whine about the pads beforehand, but be thankful after a few nasty spills) is part of the learning process. If both of you are learning together, don't be afraid to look foolish. Believe it or not, your lack of immediate success will bolster your child's opinion about learning. Setbacks won't seem so major.

If your child shows unusual dedication to the sport and wants to wear his or her skates everywhere, don't—and I know this sounds strange—discourage it (hardwood kitchen floors permitting). The sooner that being in skates feels second nature, the sooner real growth as a skater can take place. As with all things, comfort and re-

When helping a young child fasten his or her skates, seek the same snug, stable fit of your own skates.

With proper padding, even falling down (and struggling to stand up again) is a game for kids.

laxation go a long way toward success. If having a pair of skates on feels no different than walking in a pair of high-tops, the relaxation factor will be greatly increased. So if your child comes rolling into the house, or wants to roll to the school bus stop, or thinks it's great to watch TV with a pair of skates on, give her or him a little grace. The initial thrill will wear off soon enough.

Problems

The road to in-line enlightenment is not easy. We're all beset by pratfalls and physical tendencies that prevent us from becoming proficient skaters. For adults these obstacles usually come in the form of either balance problems or inability to relax. Children share the same problems, but in different ways.

Balance

Flexing the knees is a foreign concept to kids. At first, children tend to skate standing almost straight up. Their knees are locked. Their arms are either pressed straight down against the body or stretched in front of them like an apparition from a bad Frankenstein movie. Obviously, it's hard to do much more than roll and fall down from this position. Encourage your children to bend their knees (say *bend*—most won't know what *flex* means) and have them shake their arms out (make this as fun as possible) as a constant reminder to keep the arms loose. Very often, when the arms are loose, the rest of the body will follow.

Another balance problem kids have is leaning too far forward, as if bowing at the waist, but with the arms stretched out in front. They do this for a very practical reason: self-defense—any fall will be short and the arms will be there to stop it. The good side of bending at the waist is that it's impossible to lean forward on in-lines without bending the knees, so you've got one problem licked. The bad side is that you've got to find a creative way to help them lose their fear of falling. Try this: Hold them upright and walk (or skate alongside) as they get used to the sensation of skating upright. Remind them to keep their knees bent. Have them shake out those arms. If nothing else works, try having them wiggle their hips back and forth while skating. This will loosen up the lower body and remind them that they're in control, not the skates.

Muscle Development

Adults have well-developed muscles in the lower extremities, but children don't. Their bodies are still growing and lack the bulk of adult musculature. So while your ankles might have bowed inward for a short while as your legs adapted to the new feel of in-lines, a child's ankles will take that much longer to adapt because they don't have as much muscle. That's OK. If your children despair about this problem, assure them that it will be short-lived.

A good way to increase lower leg, ankle, and foot strength is by using a relatively simple training device. Begin by placing a baseball on the floor of your living room (preferably on carpet). Then, place a two-foot length of 1-by-12-inch lumber atop the ball, making an off-balance teeter-totter. After clearing the area of sharp-edged tables, breakable objects, or anything else that might cause injury in the event of a fall, help your child stand atop the piece of wood. The idea is to make the board balance atop the ball, with neither edge resting on the ground. It's harder than it sounds, and it will increase lateral muscle strength in your child's lower leg.

Why Your Kids Will Always Be Better Skaters Than You

Because it matters to them. Because adults can't spend all day during the summer rolling around in a pair of in-lines. Because not every single one of your friends has a pair (though that may be changing). Because success on in-lines can be a measure of peer acceptance. Because children are innately more physical than adults, wholly un-restrained in their love of play. Children have a way of turning work into play, and adults have a way of turning play into work. Adults often feel they have to quantify an activity, whereas children just do it (don't quantify your in-line time—its not supposed to be work).

But most of all, your children will always be better skaters than you because in-line skating is a metaphor for childhood. Its freedom and effortlessness are sensations akin to how children float through every day, and therein lies its appeal for all of us.

Take your children skating today. They will thank you.

13

BALANCE

I mentioned in the first chapter that the metaphor of balance runs through in-line skating. It is a casual sport, one that fits simply into participants' lives. There is little need for the intense hours of dedicated training that so many other sports require. No, in-lining is a sport that doubles more as a pastime, something that comes along to help while away hours or increase the enjoyment of an already great day. There is a tendency to try to quantify so much in life these days, what with the greater emphasis on quality time and other such abstract concepts that threaten to rob life of its simple joys.

In-lining defies all that. It is an easy sport, a simple sport; some would even say a trivial sport—and that's good, because life needs a little more trivia. We need a few more things that are fun for no other reason than that they are. Too often the urge with a sport, with a hobby, with anything, really, is to somehow strive to quantify that element of enjoyment in an effort to harness control. Maybe this urge is somehow an effort to duplicate this sensation of pleasure in another realm—that by figuring out what makes us so happy in one sport, it can be transferred intact to another—or perhaps just the continuous need for control that often permeates daily life. When it comes to stress-increasing sensations, nothing is higher on the list than lack of control. When we have a lack of control, we feel hemmed in and powerless. When we have control of a situation, the stress that comes with it often dissipates immediately.

This attitude toward control makes for an interesting conundrum in regards to in-line skating. On the one hand, it's a sport that requires control of all kinds to avoid calamity: precise muscle controls, control of turning radius, control of body angle and weight distribution, control of the skating environment to avoid somehow skating over a too-high chunk of sidewalk or into an open manhole. Without that control there are crashes, abrasions, contusion, confusion, hurt feelings about the sport in general, and worse feelings about your inability to master what appears to be such a simple sport when the neighborhood kids practice it. On the other hand, the most blissful moments with in-line skating come when the sensation of control is stripped away—suspended—and the possibility for calamity seems to exist, but without the accompanying fear. How wonderful it is to skate headlong down a hill, knowing in the back of your mind that a crash is entirely possible, but knowing that you are adept enough to negate the likelihood of it ever occurring. This is what balance is all about.

Control

One balance of in-line skating is that need to be in control at all times, always watchful, always diligent, if only in the depths of your subconscious. For the chance of crashing is always there, but so are the ingrained muscle memories that remind you to lean your weight forward or back, bend a knee, tilt your head—basically, do whatever it takes to create an arena of body balance necessary for optimal in-line skating.

The other balance of in-line skating is to forget that you are in control at all. You know why? Because you're not. It's really just an illusion. There are so many things that can go wrong as you skate headlong for the puck or scamper down a steep hill. You could hit a big rock that you somehow didn't see. You could have a screw pop loose from your frame and lodge in your wheels. Horror of horrors, your frame and boot could come undone, sending you in-line skating without wheels. Sure, these are extreme situations, almost guaranteed never to happen, but they underscore a vital point: The sensation of control is an illusion. Don't try to quantify it. Don't try to recreate it. Simply relax and know that in-line skating is fun, and leave it at that.

Balance.

Compulsion

Somewhere in your heart of hearts, you may get the compulsion to get compulsive. You will begin to feel bad—worse, guilty—if you skip a day's skate. You will begin to feel fatter than you really are, maybe as a result of not burning off a few extra calories. Maybe you'll feel sluggish as well, resigned to life (maybe again) as a couch potato, destined to channel surf, drink beer, and munch potato chips, all because you didn't skate.

I have two responses to that. First, channel surfing, drinking beer, and munching potato chips are likable pastimes, and I recommend them highly—in moderation. There is relaxation to be found on a comfortable sofa, especially on a Sunday afternoon when the tube is full of sports or old movies. Of course, sitting in front of the TV all day, every day, is silly. It's mind-numbing, slothful, and a less-than-diligent way to live. As Dean Wormer said in the movie *National Lampoon's Animal House:* "Fat, drunk, and stupid is no way to go through life."

My second response is that too much in-line skating can be just as mind-numbing as being a permanent couch potato. Sure, being fit is a great thing, and having a really low heart rate is terrific. But people who live to be fit—instead of being fit to *live*—are, in a word, dull. Have you ever stood next to a fitness geek at a party, and all he or she can talk about is the next day's workout? Yawn. Who needs it? If you're going to be an in-line skater, be an in-line skater because you love to in-line skate. Do it when you feel like it. Skate because you are moved to skate, not when some guilt complex you've fashioned out of old insecurities about body shape calls to you while you lie happily prone on the couch.

Balance.

Expense

There is a way to spend a lot of money on in-line skating. There is a gizmo for every need, a need for every gizmo, and a chicken in every pot. In short, there are entrepreneurs out there, nice enough guys with the forethought to design, make, and market an innovation that more than likely will do nothing whatsoever to increase the quality of life for anyone but themselves. That's the nature of a market economy, and it's not entirely a bad thing. Entrepreneurs are to be applauded, especially by in-line skaters, because as the entire sport of in-line skating was the result of a pair of entrepreneurs tinkering with a dubious invention in their basement.

However—and this is a very important *however*—the joy of in-line skating lies in simplicity. There is no need to buy a product merely because wonderful, four-color marketing brochures tell you so. There are very few things you require for the optimal in-line skating session. There's you. There's your skates, which come with wheels and buckles and a liner. And there are the pads you've chosen to wear, simply because you forgot to one day when you were feeling mildly rebellious ("What do I need pads for? I never fall") and proceeded to scrape and bang several key joints and favorite patches of skin. That's all you need.

One look through a skating catalog will tell you otherwise, of course. You'll see products you didn't know existed, but now cannot do without. Forget about them. There is a low-end side to in-lining. That means not indulging yourself foolishly, just because you've convinced yourself you need several new items. That means don't buy high-end skates that don't match your abilities, either. Or four pairs of skates when one—maybe two if you play hockey or three if you speed skate as well—is all you need.

Balance.

Philosophy

I hope that you've enjoyed this book and found things of worth to you. More so, I hope that in-line skating is something you've found yourself enjoying. Be honest with yourself as you grow into being an in-line skater. If you find yourself taking to the sport, ride that wave of enthusiasm to become the best skater you can possibly be. But don't make it your life. This is just skating, after all. It's just gliding around pavement with wheels attached to your feet. Don't give it a significance it shouldn't have.

I don't mean not to look for meaning in what you're doing. There's a Tao of skating, just as there is of running, that brings out a sense of tranquility. But instead of going inward to explore reasons and ways of controlling this peace in order to duplicate it somewhere else, go inward to enjoy the moment. Use skating as a means of exploring the inner you instead of using the inner you to look for metaphysical enlightenment in skating (or fly fishing, or running, or whatever), as many are wont to do. Remember, in-lining is just you with wheels attached to your feet. Nothing deep or significant about that.

And when the day comes that in-line skating is no longer your cup of tea, have the good sense to move on to a new sport or passion. Don't cling to in-lining out of some weird obligation, as is often the case when people have invested time, money and their physical acumen in something. A connection with your skates is not the same as connecting with a loved one, so don't feel as if the day you set aside your skates is a day for mourning or feeling otherwise inappropriate. There's no joy in skating out of obligation. Skate until you can skate no more, then find some other way to sharpen a talent you've always wondered if you owned. As the author of a how-to book, I feel that's the best advice I can give.

Of course, I hope you enjoy skating for a long, long time and that the day when your skates no longer call to you is far away. In the meantime, I pray that your skating is safe and wondrously simple.

Balance.

Appendix

Equipment Manufacturers

ATOMIC/OXYGEN
9 Columbia Drive, Amherst, NH 33999; (603) 880–6143

BAUER CANSTAR
50 Jonergin Drive, Swanton, VT 05488; (802) 868–2711

BULL'Z EYE
111 Broadway Avenue, Costa Mesa, CA 92627; (714) 373–2535

CCM/MASKA U.S.
7405 TransCanada Highway, St. Laurent, QU H4T–1Z2;
(514) 331–5150

EASTON SPORTS
577 Airport Boulevard, Burlingame, CA 94010; (415) 347–4727

EXEL MARKETING/ROCES
One Second Street, Peabody, MA 01960; (508) 532–2226

HILLERICH & BRADSBY/LOUISVILLE HOCKEY
14 Arnold Street, Wallaceburg, ONT N8A3P4; (519) 627–2248

HYPER CORPORATION
3731 West Warner, Santa Ana, CA 92704; (714) 850–8800

KARHU USA INC/KOHO
55 Green Mountain Drive, South Burlington, VT 05403;
(802) 884–4519

KRYPTONICS
740 South Pierce, Louisville, CO 80027; (310) 448–7357

K2 CORPORATION
19215 Vashon Highway S.W., Vashon, WA 98070; (802) 884–4519

KUZAK
13315 Washington Boulevard, Los Angeles, CA 90066;
(310) 448–7357

MISSION ROLLER HOCKEY
201 East Stevens, Santa Ana, CA 92707; (714) 556–8856

MYLEC
Mill Circle Road, Winchester, MA 01477; (508) 297–0089

ROLLERBLADE, INC.
5101 Shady Oak Road, Minnetonka, MN 55343; (800) 328–0171

SUN HOCKEY, INC.
Box 36155, Edina, MN 55435; (612) 935–9140

TECNICA, USA
19 Technology Drive, West Lebanon, NH 03784; (603) 298–8032

ULTRAWHEELS
1201 Lund Boulevard, Anoka, MN 55303; (612) 578–3500

Professional Leagues and National Series

CONTINENTAL IN-LINE HOCKEY LEAGUE
44-100 Monterey Avenue, Palm Desert, CA 92260; (619) 836–3434

NATIONAL IN-LINE HOCKEY ASSOCIATION
999 Brickell Avenue, 9th Floor, Miami, FL 33131; (800) 358–6442

NATIONAL IN-LINE SKATE SERIES
11661 San Vicente Boulevard, Los Angeles, CA 90049;
(310) 828–5464

NATIONAL HOCKEY LEAGUE BREAKOUT TOUR
4006 Belt Line Road, Dallas, TX 75244; (214) 404–1999

ROLLER HOCKEY INTERNATIONAL
150-B South Auburn Street, Grass Valley, CA 94945;
(916) 272–7825

In-Line Skating Magazines

INLINE HOCKEY NEWS
710 Wilshire Boulevard, Suite 235, Santa Monica, CA 90401; (310)
656-7531. Hockeyrg@aol.com

IN-LINE SKATER
4099 Mcewen Drive, Suite 350, Dallas, TX 75244-5039

INLINE
2025 Pearl Street, Boulder, CO 80302; (303) 440-5111

BOX
2025 Pearl Street, Boulder, CO 80302; (303) 440-5111

IN-LINE RETAILER & INDUSTRY NEWS
2025 Pearl Street, Boulder, CO 80302; (303) 440-5111

SKATER
660 Venice Boulevard, Suite 165, Venice, CA 90291; (310) 827-
5242

GLOBAL SKATE
16478 Beach Boulevard, Suite 361, Westminster, CA 92683;
(714)379-6555

HOCKEY AND SKATING
701J Delaney Avenue, Novato, CA 94945; (415) 898-5414

IN-LINE SKATERMAG
The Blue Barn, Wooton, Woodstock, OXON OX2O 1HA, England

Index

About the Author

Martin Dugard is a freelance writer whose stories about extreme and endurance sports have appeared in such publications as *Sports Illustrated, GQ,* and *Outside.* As editor of *California City Sports* magazine for two years, he wrote and edited articles on in-line skating, in-line hockey, cycling, and running.

He was the only American journalist invited to report on the prestigious *Raid Gauloises* in Madagascar in 1992 and has covered the race each year ever since, giving the sport of adventure racing its name. He is also co-holder of the around-the-world speed record, having traveled from New York to New York in a little more than thirty-one hours in 1995.

Mr. Dugard lives with his wife and two boys in Southern California, where he has been skating for some twenty-one years.